The Handyman's Dictionary

Derek Hall

The Handyman's Dictionary

Illustrated by
Jackson Day Designs

Stanley Paul
London Melbourne Sydney Auckland Johannesburg

For all reluctant do-it-yourselfers

Stanley Paul & Co. Ltd

An imprint of the Hutchinson Publishing Group

3 Fitzroy Square, London W1P 6JD

Hutchinson Group (Australia) Pty Ltd
30–32 Cremorne Street, Richmond South, Victoria 3121
PO Box 151, Broadway, New South Wales 2007

Hutchinson Group (NZ) Ltd
32–34 View Road, PO Box 40–086, Glenfield, Auckland 10

Hutchinson Group (SA) (Pty) Ltd
PO Box 337, Bergvlei 2012, South Africa

First published 1980

© Derek Hall 1980

Set in Linotron Times

Printed and bound in Great Britain
at The Pitman Press, Bath

British Library Cataloguing in Publication Data
Hall, Derek
    The handyman's dictionary.
    1. Dwellings – Maintenance and repair – Amateurs'
    manuals
    I. Title
    643'.7   TH4817.3

ISBN 0 09 142220 5 (cased)
ISBN 0 09 142221 3 (paper)

Preface

'Boy! Get me some more toast!' . . . 'Hey, you! Put a couple of bob each way on Moby Dick for me, willya!'

I was a 14½-year-old Fleet Street 'runner', being bawled at by everybody from copy editors to door porters, but at least I understood what they were talking about. When, many years later, I started studying architecture and spent some time working on building sites, I was never quite sure whether I was being got at or not. 'Go get me an air brick, will you?' . . . 'fetch us a couple of noggins' . . . 'help Tommo measure up his dead leg' . . . 'ask Mick if I can borrow his mouse' . . . and, perhaps the worst of all, 'like to join 'Arry on the roof, and do a bit of flashing?'

It was all very bewildering. The newcomer to do-it-yourself – whether as an inexperienced householder or someone putting up a shelf for the first time – is likely to be equally confused by the argot. Most trades and professions have evolved a language of their own – a practice that harks back to the middle ages when men jealously guarded their newly-won skills and preserved their secrets from outsiders by forming guilds and masonic lodges.

The purpose of this book, therefore, is to help the newcomer to understand the language (or jargon, as many would prefer to call it) of the experts – the architects . . . the builders . . . the surveyors . . . and the many craftsmen and tradesmen involved in building and servicing houses.

As well as an aid to understanding what

experts are talking about, the book will be a help when reading builders' documents, such as specifications, contracts, estimates and invoices, in addition to manufacturers' sales and technical literature. It will also help the newcomer to identify many of the materials, tools and fittings that are available and, in most cases, explain what they are used for.

I should also like to think it will be an *aide-mémoire* to the experienced.

Some readers find the inevitable cross-referencing in a dictionary fascinating: it leads them to other definitions and subjects and thereby adds to their interest; others (and I confess to being one of them) find it irritating. To those like me, I offer my apologies, for it was my original intention to produce a dictionary that would be free of cross-referencing. However, I rapidly discovered that such a system would have made the book twice as thick and more expensive. Consequently, although all subjects have their own separate entry, some have their definitions grouped together under a major entry. For example, all hammers are listed under their various names, *Claw, Club, Cross-pein, Engineer's, Sledge* and *Veneer* hammers; but all are cross-referenced to a major entry under **Hammers**.

Similarly, there are several tools – and a few techniques – that share two or more different names. A *Backsaw*, a *Gent's Saw* and a *Dovetail Saw* can all be one and the same tool. In such cases, the alternative names will have been given their own entry, with a cross-reference to the definition listed under the most popular name. Wherever relevant, the end of an entry has cross-references to other definitions of equal or associated interest.

Where a tool, fitting or item of material has a metric measurement assigned to it – not all sections of the building industry have yet gone over to the 'new' system – they have been given, with their exact or nearest imperial equivalent. These will be seen to vary in many cases due to manufacturers choosing to 'round up' rather than 'down' (and vice-versa) when selecting equivalent values.

In conclusion, more than twenty-five years' experience of architecture and building has left me only too well aware of how vast the scope of do-it-yourself now is. In drawing up the contents of this book, therefore, I have had to be ruthlessly selective, perhaps choosing some entries that some readers would disagree with, and leaving out others that some might feel to have been essential. I hope that I have managed to achieve the right balance, but I would be grateful to hear suggestions from any readers who feel seriously about an omission – as well as any mistakes that may have crept in – so that any possible future edition can be suitably rectified.

Derek Hall
London

Bibliography

'A man will turn over half a library to make a book' – so said Dr Johnson, the king of lexicographers. Certainly, in my time both as a student and a professional, I have read, referred to, or rifled my way through a great many books on architecture, building, do-it-yourself and other related subjects.

Some of these books are old favourites, regularly revised and reprinted to remain as reliable works of reference. Others, although relatively new arrivals, have nevertheless rapidly established themselves as authoritative books. The selection of works listed below is offered to the reader with confidence – ranging from those useful to the inexperienced beginners to those consulted by professionals.

Complete Do-it-yourself Manual, Repair Manual, Book of Home Improvements, Reader's Digest

Do-it-yourself Book, David Day and Albert Jackson, Good Housekeeping

The Home Handyman Encyclopaedia, Harold King, Octopus

Home Heating, B. J. King and J. E. Beer, Teach Yourself

The Practical Plumbing Guide, James M. Haig, Stanley Paul

Home Lighting, Anthony Byers, Pelham Books

Electricity Supply and Safety, Edith Rudinger, Consumers' Association

Let's Decorate, Roy Day, ICI

Power Tool Carpentry, Black & Decker, Marshall Cavendish

BIBLIOGRAPHY

Painting & Decoration, L. F. J. Tubb

Plumbing, F. Hall, Macmillan

A Concise Building Encyclopaedia, T. Corkhill, Pitman

A Dictionary Of Building, John S. Scott, Penguin

The Complete Book of Tools, Albert Jackson and David Day, Michael Joseph

Building Materials, Cecil C. Handisyde, Building Elements, R. L. Davies and D. J. Petty, Architectural Press

Mitchell's Building Construction – Advanced & Elementary, Raymond Moxley and Denzil Nield, Batsford

Specification, Dex Harrison, Architectural Press

Acknowledgments

The seeds of this book were originally sown in collaboration with Garry Porter, Architect, RIBA, FFAS, who illustrated a smaller version of *The Handyman's Dictionary* that was originally published in *Do It Yourself* magazine. I am grateful therefore to the editor, Tony Wilkins, for his permission to use the original version as a basis for this dictionary, and to his editorial staff, headed by John McGowan, for their unfailing courtesy and willingness to help on the many occasions I have pestered them for factual information.

For the same reason I also acknowledge help give to me by staff at the London Building Centre, Ferguson Ramsay & Co. Ltd (ONI hinges), and Messrs Woodfit Ltd (furniture, fittings and fitments).

I should like to thank Robin Harris for his illustrations and David Day and Albert Jackson for their co-operation – their splendid publication *The Complete Book of Tools* proved to be a unique work of reference.

Special thanks are due to Garry Porter, whose tenacity as a checker and twenty-five years of friendship I have reason to value.

Finally, no man with a wife and two small children can hope to write a reference book without their co-operation. As far as my family have been concerned, the word 'dictionary' is synonymous with 'isolationism' – shutting myself away to live like a hermit. To Val, Spencer and Serena . . . thank you.

ABRASIVES Materials used for cleaning, smoothing, shaping or polishing surfaces such as wood, metal, plaster or paintwork. Most abrasives are available in textures ranging from fine to extra coarse, and are generally coded accordingly.

Emery Paper or cloth backed with fine particles of carborundum – a hard, crystallized mineral. Emery is used chiefly for finishing metal and can be used with water to reduce dust.

Garnet Paper backed with finely powdered garnet – a natural mineral. Garnet paper is suitable for hand finishing most timbers, including hardwood, and is sold in finer textures than glasspaper.

Glasspaper Often wrongly referred to as 'sandpaper' (which does not exist), it consists of fine particles of glass and flint glued to paper. Cheapest of the abrasive papers, glasspaper is used for giving a reasonably smooth finish to wood. It wears out quickly.

Steel wool A versatile abrasive consisting of filaments of steel, ranging in texture from fine to coarse, packed into pads – some impregnated with soap. Steel wool is useful for cleaning and polishing metals – particularly aluminium – for smoothing woodwork and for removing stains from plastic flooring materials.

Wet and dry The popular name for a waterproof paper, backed with a synthetic material, silicon carbide, that is harder than emery. The abrasive can be used dry, like glasspaper, on wood, or wet for smoo-

thing old paintwork before repainting, or cleaning rust stains from metal.
(◆ POWER TOOL ATTACHMENTS)

ACCESS EYE ◆ RODDING EYE

ACOUSTIC INSULATION ◆ INSULATING MATERIALS

ACOUSTIC TILES Square or rectangular tiles, made of sound-absorbent materials with smooth, rough, grooved or perforated surfaces. Some types of tiles need decorating, but the easiest to use are those with a natural finish.

Acoustic tiles, when applied to walls and ceilings, deaden the sounds made within a room but do not effectively muffle external noises.

ACRYLIC PAINT ◆ PAINT

ACTIVATED CHARCOAL The material used for filters in cooker hoods that regenerates the air in a kitchen. An electrically driven fan sucks the air through the filters, which absorb grease and fumes.

The filters usually need replacing every twelve to eighteen months, according to the amount of time the hood is in use.

ADAPTOR (Electric) A fitting that enables two appliances to be plugged into a single SOCKET OUTLET. Adaptors should be used with care; it is dangerous to use appliances that consume more electricity than the socket is rated to supply. Thus, a 13 amp socket outlet can supply up to 3000 WATTS – to use more, is likely to fuse or damage the socket, adaptor, or cause a fire.

ADHESIVES The range of adhesives available to the handyman is enormous: there are literally scores of different brand names, as well as a great many proprietary adhesives made for specific purposes, such as fixing ceramic or vinyl floor tiles, various wall coverings and expanded polystyrene products.

Each type of adhesive has its own special characteristics, e.g. what it is best suited for, its strength properties, methods of application and setting time, etc. In all cases, manufacturers' instructions should be observed closely.

A selection of the most common types of adhesive are as follows:

Animal A traditional adhesive (which includes Scotch glue) made from animal and fish bones and other natural substances, such as vegetable or tree resins.

It is a strong glue, but is slow to set and has a poor resistance to moisture. Can be used for wood, glass, china and pottery, fabrics, card and paper.

Sold as a powder to be mixed with water, in beads to be heated in water, and in ready-to-use liquid form.

Contact (impact) Strong adhesive used primarily for sticking sheet materials such as plywood or plastic laminates, but also suitable for many household repairs. Not good for highly stressed joints.

Thin layers of adhesive are applied to both surfaces and left until 'touch-dry' before being brought together. They bond instantly and therefore precision placing is essential.

Thixotropic contact adhesive is available – a non-drip glue for overhead work.

Sold in containers for instant use.

Epoxy resin One of the strongest and most versatile of all adhesives, it makes a waterproof and heat-resistant bond. It can be used for most materials in common use, such as concrete, earthenware, glass, metal, rubber and wood, and for some plastics.

It is expensive and therefore more economical for small repairs.

Sold in twin-pack containers: a resin and a hardener in separate tubes which must be mixed in equal parts before use. Work must be cramped together until the adhesive is set – up to six hours.

General-purpose A cellulose-based clear

adhesive, ideal for a range of small and light household repairs. It is not always permanent and – with some materials – not as efficient as a specialized adhesive. But it dries transparent and sets quickly – an advantage where cramping the surfaces may not be practical.

Latex A rubber-based adhesive that is primarily used for sticking fabrics to themselves and where a strong, flexible bond is required, such as carpet work and upholstery. Suitable for leather and cardboard.

Has a white, creamy consistency when wet but dries transparent and sets rapidly. Sold in tubes and jars.

PVA (Polyvinyl acetate) An ideal adhesive for woodwork but unsuitable for outdoor use or where an article may be subject to damp conditions.

A milky-looking fluid, it is applied thinly to both surfaces, which must be cramped together until dry – from thirty minutes to six hours according to the brand.

It is sold in flexible containers. *Synthetic resin (Urea-formaldehyde)* An exceptionally strong adhesive for all interior and exterior woodwork, it is heat-resistant, waterproof and dries transparent.

Sold as a powder that must be mixed with water, or as a fluid in a twin-pack; separate liquids must be mixed together first. A thin layer of adhesive is applied to one surface only and the two must be cramped together until set – about three hours.

ADJUSTABLE SPANNER ♦ SPANNERS

ADJUSTABLE WRENCH ♦
WRENCHES

AGGREGATE The material that is mixed with cement to make mortar or concrete and give them their bulk and strength.

Fine aggregate is SAND; coarse aggregate is gravel, crushed gravel or crushed

4

stone, usually graded from 5 mm ($\frac{3}{16}$ in.) to a maximum of 20 mm ($\frac{3}{4}$ in.).

The choice of aggregate and the ratio of the mixture vary according to the strength, character and appearance of the mortar or concrete required; often the larger the mass the larger the aggregate used.

An 'all-in' aggregate can be bought from many builders' merchants and is a mixture of aggregate and sand made up in the correct proportions to suit a specific job.

AIR BRICK ◆ BRICKS

AIR CHAMBER A pipe of larger diameter than the RISING MAIN that is fixed at the head of the pipe, where it supplies a COLD WATER STORAGE CISTERN, in order to combat the effects of WATER HAMMER. The air in the chamber acts as a 'spring', contracting and expanding to absorb the shock created by compressed air in the pipework.

AIR CHANGES Air must circulate in a house in order to maintain conditions of comfort and health. The number of times the air in a room should be replaced to achieve these conditions is expressed as so many air changes per hour.

Kitchens, bathrooms and lavatories are generally given ten to fifteen air changes per hour; the remainder of a house is given one to one and a half air changes.

AIR LOCK Air trapped in a plumbing system, creating erratic water flow and knocking noises in the pipework.
(◆ AIR VENT)

AIR VENT A valve that releases the air in a radiator when it is being filled with water or when an AIR LOCK is preventing it from heating efficiently.

An air vent may have an automatic valve fitted in it, or it can be opened with a square-ended key.

ALLEN KEYS L-shaped, hexagonal rods of steel, used to tighten or loosen

recessed screw heads or bolt heads of corresponding sizes.

Allen keys are made in varying sizes up to 15 mm diameter.

ALUMINIUM FOIL ♦ INSULATION MATERIAL

AMPERE (Amp) The unit used to measure the flow of electricity through a cable or wire.

ANAGLYPTA ♦ WALL COVERINGS

ANCHOR BOLT A steel bolt that can be set in brickwork, lightweight concrete blocks or concrete to provide a rigid fixing for timber or metalwork. Many types of anchor bolt are made, some for fixing in pre-drilled holes, others for casting in concrete, but all conform to a similar principle. The tail of the bolt has a steel, rubber or plastic sleeve that expands, by the action of a wedge-shaped nut, when a lock nut is tightened.

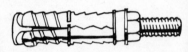

Anchor bolts are manufactured in a variety of lengths, and are generally available from 5 mm to 32 mm ($\frac{3}{16}$ in. to $1\frac{1}{4}$ in.) in diameter.

Also known as a rag bolt.

ANGLE BEAD A right-angled strip of galvanized metal, with wings of expanded mesh, used to reinforce the plastered corners of brickwork. See right.

The mesh is fixed to the brickwork with dabs of plaster.

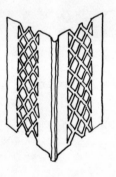

ANGLE TILES Specially moulded tiles for corner situations, such as for skirtings made of clay or ceramic tiles, or for roof tiling.

ANGLE TROWEL A metal trowel with its edges turned up at right angles. It is used by plasterers to achieve a smooth finish on corner situations.

Sizes of blades are 90 mm by 50 mm ($3\frac{1}{2}$ ins. by 2 ins.).

ANIMAL GLUE ♦ ADHESIVES

ANNULAR NAIL ♦ NAILS

ANODIZING A hard film of protective oxide given to aluminium by artificial (electro-chemical) methods. The finish can be matt or glossy, or dyed to a range of metallic-looking colours.

ANTI-CONDENSATION PAINT ♦ PAINT

ANTI-SIPHONAGE PIPE A small-bore pipe, used in some plumbing systems, that admits air to the waste pipes from a water closet, basin or bath to prevent the water in a trap being siphoned off.

(♦ TRAPS)

ANTIQUE ♦ GLASS

APRON FLASHING Sheet metal (copper, lead or zinc) cut and shaped to weatherproof the lowest point where a vertical surface passes through a roof, e.g. a chimney stack or window.

(♦ FLASHINGS)

ARCHITRAVE Plain or moulded lengths of timber that cover the joint between a door frame or door lining and the adjacent wall.

(♦ DOOR FRAME; DOOR LINING)

ARMOURPLATE ♦ GLASS

ARRIS The sharp edge formed by two surfaces meeting at an angle, e.g. the corner of a brick or stone.

ARRIS RAILS Triangular-shaped fencing rails fixed horizontally between upright posts to provide a fixing for vertical boarding.

ARRISSING The technique of smoothing the rough edges of newly cut glass with a wet and fine-textured abrasive stone.

ASBESTOS CEMENT PRODUCTS Materials consisting of asbestos fibres and Portland cement compressed and moulded into flat or corrugated sheets suitable for outside wall-cladding, roofing and rainwater goods. Sheets vary in thickness from 5 mm to 13 mm ($\frac{3}{16}$ in. to $\frac{1}{2}$ in.), and in their density and texture – some are hard

7

and brittle, others more fibrous and resilient.

Since many asbestos cement products are incombustible they are useful where fire-resisting qualities are needed, such as for lining a ceiling of a garage directly beneath a bedroom.

(◆ GUTTERS AND DOWNPIPES)

ASBESTOS VINYL ◆ PLASTIC FLOORING

ASPHALT An impervious mixture of bitumen and a large proportion of finely crushed aggregate.

Asphalt, which will not rot, is used for traditional flat roofs and lining *in situ* box gutters, for surfacing paths and drives, and for damp-proofing basements.

It can be laid hot or cold, but for most DIY purposes cold asphalt (sold in plastic bags) is convenient.

(◆ BOX GUTTERS; DAMP-PROOF COURSE; DAMP-PROOF MEMBRANE)

AUGER BIT ◆ BITS

AWL ◆ BRADAWL

BACK BOILER A boiler fitted behind an open fire or cast as an integral part of a room heater, providing hot water for domestic purposes. Some back boilers are large enough to heat water for a central heating system with a few radiators.
(◗ CENTRAL HEATING)

BACK FILL Excavated earth that is used to fill trenches after the foundations and brickwork up to ground floor level have been laid.

BACK-FLAP HINGE ◗ HINGES

BACKGROUND HEATING ◗ CENTRAL HEATING

BACK SAW ◗ SAWS

BALANCED FLUE An appliance that can be attached to a gas-fired boiler or heater to draw in fresh air and discharge exhaust fumes through the same opening.

The flue is built into an external wall and connected to the boiler or heater with an air-tight seal. The appliance, which replaces the need for a conventional chimney, has a relatively unobtrusive metal grille on the outside of the wall.

BALLAST Sand and shingle used as an AGGREGATE when making concrete.

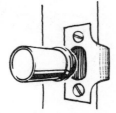

BALL CATCH A door fastening, consisting of a spring-loaded steel ball or nylon roller held in a cylinder or metal plate. As the door is closed, the ball or roller engages in a hole or recess in a corresponding fitting (KEEPER PLATE) screwed to the door frame.

Ball catches are suitable for lightweight

cupboard doors, such as those of kitchen cabinets.

BALL-PEIN HAMMER ♦ HAMMERS

BALL VALVE The flow of water into a storage cistern or lavatory flushing cistern is controlled by a valve on the end of the incoming supply pipe. The valve is operated by a lever arm, on the end of which there is a hollow copper or plastic ball which floats on the water's surface.

As the cistern empties the ball sinks and the valve opens; as the cistern fills the ball rises with the water to a predetermined level and the valve is closed.

There are several kinds of valve in use, the most common being the Croydon, Garston, Portsmouth and Equilibrium valves.

A ball valve may fail to close properly (and cause water to emerge from the relevant OVERFLOW) due to a worn rubber, nylon or fibre washer in the seat of the fitting.

BALUSTER One of the upright posts that support the handrail on a railing or staircase. The handrail and balusters are collectively known as the balustrade; less commonly, on internal staircases, they are known as the banister.

BAND SAW ♦ SAWS

BARGE BOARDS The inclined boards that seal and weatherproof the ends of the structural timbers on a gable-ended roof. Also known as verge boards.

(♦ GABLE)

BARREL BOLT A finger-operated bolt that slides back and forth within a cylindrical sleeve to secure a door. The sleeve is in two parts – one fixed to the door, the other to the frame.

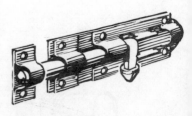

Barrel bolts are made in a wide range of sizes in brass, aluminium, steel and chromium-plated metals.

BASIN WRENCH ♦ WRENCHES

BASKET-WEAVE BOND A decorative arrangement of laying paving bricks or hardwood flooring blocks.
(◆ WOOD-BLOCK FLOORING)

BAT A brick that has been cut across its width for bonding purposes. Proportions can be quarter, half or three-quarter bats, and large or small bevelled bats.
(◆ BONDS; BRICKS)

BATTEN Lengths of sawn softwood, approximately 50 mm by 25 mm (2 ins. by 1 in.) in section, used in general purpose work such as framing jobs or fixings for wall cladding, e.g. decorative boarding.

Tiling battens, used on roofs and walls clad with slates or tiles, are generally smaller – 38 mm by 19 mm (1¾ ins. by ¾ in.).

BEADED JOINT A semi-circular moulding used in woodwork to disguise a joint.

BEADING Thin strips of plain or moulded timber – usually hardwood – used to mask joints in joinery work.

BEAM A ROLLED STEEL JOIST (RSJ), concrete LINTEL, or heavy timber, used horizontally to bridge an opening and support the weight of walls or floors above. A beam may be supported at each end or at intervals between by columns or walls, or cantilevered.

BEARER A horizontal timber which supports other timbers or a JOIST.

BED FACE The underneath surface of a brick or stone that is laid horizontally.

BENCH HOOK A flat piece of wood, with a block of wood about 25 mm (1 in.) square, screwed to each end but on opposite sides.

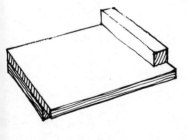

The hook is used on a bench to hold wood steady while cutting with a tenon saw.

BENCHING The sand and cement surfacing inside an INSPECTION CHAMBER (MANHOLE) that rounds off corners and forms sloping surfaces to ensure a smooth flow of the effluent discharged into and out of the chamber.

BENCH STOP A wood or metal device let into the top of a bench to provide a stop for timber to rest against while it is being planed. Retractable types can be lowered to leave the surface of the bench unobstructed.

BENDING SPRING A closely coiled steel spring that is used for bending copper or lead pipes. The correct size spring is oiled and twisted into the pipe so that a curve can be formed without distorting the walls of the pipe.

Also known as a pipe bender.

Spring sizes are available for 6 mm to 15 mm ($\frac{1}{4}$ in. to $\frac{5}{8}$ in.) nominal diameter pipes.

BEVEL An angled or splayed edge on a piece of timber.

BEVELLED EDGE CHISEL
♦ CHISELS (WOOD)

BIB TAP ♦ TAPS

BILL OF QUANTITIES A detailed breakdown – prepared by a quantity surveyor – of all the labour and materials that form part of a CONTRACT. The Bill represents an excellent method of cost control and helps to make a more accurate estimate when tendering for the contract.

BINDER The liquid part of paint, such as resins, oils or varnishes, that holds (or binds) the pigment together.

(♦ PAINTS)

BIRDSMOUTH An angled cut that resembles a bird's beak made in a piece of timber so that it can notch over another timber, e.g. where a RAFTER fits over a WALL PLATE.

BITS Different types of cutting tools, made of steel, for drilling holes in metal or wood. Some are suitable for use in a brace, others in hand or power drills. Of the wide range of bits available, each has its own characteristics. Those commonly used by the handyman are:

Centre Used with a brace for drilling holes in wood. It has a lead (starting) screw head and two helical cutting edges – one with a spur-point that scribes a circle, the other that ploughs out the wood.

Sizes from 100 mm to 150 mm (4 ins. to 6 ins.) long, and 6 mm to 56 mm ($\frac{1}{4}$ in. to $2\frac{1}{4}$ ins.) diameter.

Countersink A bit with a cone-shaped cutting end, used in a brace, so that the head of a countersunk screw will fit flush when driven home. A 'high-speed bit' is available for power-drill work.

Sizes are 9 mm, 13 mm and 16 mm ($\frac{3}{8}$ in., $\frac{1}{2}$ in. and $\frac{5}{8}$ in.) diameters.

Dowel Used in a power drill to make a flat-bottomed hole for dowelling.

Sizes from 3 mm to 13 mm ($\frac{1}{8}$ in. to $\frac{1}{2}$ in.) diameters.

Expansive Similar to a centre bit but with an adjustable head for drilling different size holes.

Sizes from 13 mm to 75 mm ($\frac{1}{2}$ in. to 3 in.) diameters.

Jennings (Auger) Has a double helix cutting edge that clears out waste material as it penetrates the wood. Also has a lead (starting) screw head.

Sizes from 200 mm to 250 mm (8 ins. to 10 ins.) long and 6 mm to 38 mm ($\frac{1}{4}$ in. to $1\frac{1}{2}$ ins.) diameters.

Masonry Steel bit with a hardened tip of tungsten carbide, suitable for drilling holes in brickwork, concrete, masonry or ceramic tiles. Can be used in hand or power drills.

Sizes from 3 mm to 25 mm ($\frac{1}{8}$ in. to 1 in.) diameters.

Plug cutter A cylindrically shaped cutter, for use with a power drill, to cut out plugs of matching timber for concealing screw holes in good class joinery.

Sizes match the sizes of dowel bits.

13

Screwdriver Varied types of double-headed screwdriver tips are available to fit HAND DRILLS.

Spear-point A steel bit, tipped with tungsten carbide, for drilling holes in glass or porcelain.

Sizes 3 mm to 13 mm ($\frac{1}{8}$ in. to $\frac{1}{2}$ in.) diameters.

Tank cutter A cutting bit that combines a twist drill – for centring – with a larger diameter serrated blade for cutting larger diameter holes in thin metal, such as a water storage tank. The bits are available in a range of sizes and are intended for use in a brace.

Twist Used in hand or power drills for making holes in wood or metalwork.

Range of sizes from 1.5 mm to 13 mm ($\frac{1}{16}$ in. to $\frac{1}{2}$ in.) diameters.

BITUMINOUS FELT Fibrous materials, such as hessian, flax or asbestos, sandwiched and bonded together in two or three layers with bitumen – a tar-like mineral – to make a weatherproof covering for roofing. Some felts are finished with a layer of marble or stone chippings set in hot bitumen. Made in 1 m wide rolls and of varying thicknesses.

BITUMINOUS PAINT ◗ PAINTS

BLEACHING The loss of original colour strength that occurs in some materials, such as unpainted wood or paintwork, when exposed to the combined effects of sunlight and atmosphere. More likely to occur in strong, dark colours than in light ones.

BLEEDING Blemishes in paintwork caused by natural resins, or soluble or bituminous substances in undercoats passing through the top coat.

(◗ KNOTTING; SEALERS)

BLIND NAILING ◗ SECRET NAILING

BLISTERING Paintwork that is disfigured by moisture trapped beneath the film of paint expanding in warm weather.

14

Can be the result of painting woodwork during damp weather.

BLOCKBOARD A strong, manufactured board with a core of 25 mm (1 in.) wide strips of softwood, glued and bonded together under pressure and sandwiched between one or two veneers of hardwood.

The grain of the core and the veneers are at right angles to each other to give added strength.

Blockboard is made in a range of sheet sizes, e.g. 2440 mm by 1220 mm (8 ft by 4 ft), and in thicknesses varying from 12 mm to 32 mm ($\frac{1}{2}$ in. to $1\frac{1}{4}$ ins.).

BLOCK PLANE ♦ PLANES

BLOW LAMP A paraffin-fuelled lamp, useful for burning off old paintwork or brazing or soldering metal.

The modern equivalent is gas-fuelled – using either butane or propane – and is easier to control. The fuel is contained in pressurized cartridges or cannisters which are screwed or clipped on to the burner and so form the body of the lamp.

Blow torches are more expensive but easier to handle and have a higher heat output. They consist of a hand-held burner, linked by a length of hose to a gas cylinder.

Most types of lamps can be fitted with alternative burners to vary the intensity and spread of the flame.

BLOW TORCH ♦ BLOW LAMP

BOILER A water heater, fuelled by solid fuel, gas, oil or electricity. A boiler either heats water for domestic purposes or is part of a central heating system.

(♦ BACK BOILER; CENTRAL HEATING; IMMERSION HEATER)

BOLSTER ♦ CHISELS 'METAL'

BOLT CUTTER A lever-action, shear-like tool, which can exert sufficient force to cut through steel bolts and rods from 6 mm to 16 mm ($\frac{1}{4}$ in. to $\frac{5}{8}$ in.) in diameter.

BONDS Varied arrangements of laying bricks together to form a strong and stable wall. Each bond presents a different appearance on the outer face.

Since the strengths of most bonds are comparable they are usually chosen primarily for their appearance, although some bonds require more bricks per cubic metre than others and may therefore be more costly.

The principal bonds are:

english

English The bricks are laid in alternate COURSES (rows) of HEADERS and STRETCHERS to form the strongest of all brickwork bonds.

English garden wall The bricks are laid to show three courses of stretchers and one course of headers, alternately.

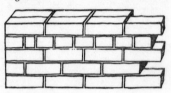

english garden wall

Flemish The bricks are laid to show staggered courses of alternate stretchers and headers.

Honeycomb Sometimes known as open bond, it has a half-brick wall (i.e. 102 mm (4⅛ ins. thick) laid with spaces between the stretchers and lining up vertically in alternate courses.

The bond is used for SLEEPER WALLS or for decorative garden walling.

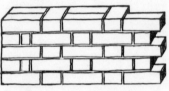

flemish

Rat-trap The bricks are laid on edge to form two walls with a form of cavity between them, linked by headers. Stretchers are laid between the headers and alternate courses line up vertically. The bond is fairly strong and inexpensive but it is not used for conventional CAVITY WALLS.

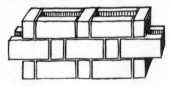

rat trap

Stretcher Used to build a wall that is half a brick thick, i.e. 102 mm, showing stretchers only. This bond is used on the outer face of CAVITY WALLS.

(♦ BASKET-WEAVE; HERRING-BONE)

BOTTLE TRAP ♦ TRAPS

BOW SAW ♦ SAWS

BOX GUTTER A gutter, formed IN SITU, between a parapet wall and an adjacent flat or sloping roof, or two adjacent

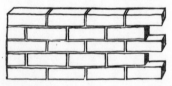

stretcher

roofs, or between a roof and an adjacent wall.

The gutter is usually framed and surfaced with softwood, laid to slope towards an outlet pipe and lined with a waterproof material, such as ASPHALT.

BOX JOINT Also known variously as finger or comb joint, it is used in making built-in fittings and lightweight furniture as an easier alternative to cutting a DOVETAIL JOINT.

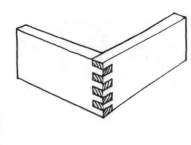

BOX SPANNER ♦ SPANNERS

BRACE ♦ DRILLS

BRACKET A right-angled support, made in wood or metal, to carry the weight of a projecting surface, such as a shelf or balcony.

Brackets are also the small, rough pieces of wood nailed to the CARRIAGE (sloping support) on a staircase, helping to keep the TREADS and RISERS rigid.
(♦ STAIRCASE)

BRADAWL A small hand tool used for making starting holes in wood before screwing, fixing cup hooks, etc. It is also used for piercing holes in leather.

The tip of the tool may be pointed or squared, like a screwdriver.

BREAST DRILL ♦ DRILLS

BRICKLAYER'S LINE AND PINS Also known as line pins, they are used by bricklayers to ensure that new brickwork is built straight and level.

There is a pair of pins, about 75 mm (3 ins.) long, with large heads and flat, blade-shaped ends, and nylon line, 9 m to 18 m (about 9½ yds to 19½ yds) long. A pin is pushed into the damp mortar at each end of the wall, with the line stretched taut between them.

BRICKLAYER'S TROWELS There are two basic types:

Bricklayer's The traditional tool used to hand mix mortar on a SPOT BOARD and apply mortar to bricks or concrete blocks.

The diamond-shaped blade may be left-
or right-handed, with one straight edge and
one slightly curved – hardened to cut
bricks.

Blade lengths vary from 165 mm to
300 mm (roughly 6½ ins. to 12 ins.).

Pointing A smaller version of the above –
with blade lengths from 75 mm to 200 mm
(3 ins. to 8 ins.) – used for the finer work
required when pointing, i.e. finishing the
mortar joints between bricks.

BRICK-ON-EDGE A method of
finishing the top of a 225 mm (9 ins.) thick
wall, with the last COURSE of bricks laid on
edge across the wall.

The end bricks are sometimes given
additional anchorage with a small length of
mild steel angle.

BRICKS Convenient-sized rectangular
blocks of burnt clay, they vary enormously
in colour, texture, appearance and purpose, according to the type of clay used.
Bricks may also be hand- or machine-
made.

Scores of different shapes and types are
made to suit specific purposes, but a selection of the more common bricks used in
housing are as follows:

Air brick A perforated brick built into a
wall to ventilate a room, a disused and
otherwise sealed chimney flue, the space
beneath a SUSPENDED FLOOR, or the
space between the inner and outer leaves
of a CAVITY WALL.

Bullnose Bricks having one or more rounded corners that are suitable for finishing
the tops or ends of walls.

Common (or *Fletton*) A relatively inexpensive brick used primarily for its strength
rather than its appearance. It is however
prone to frost damage and is therefore
usually protected, when used externally,
with RENDERING, ROUGHCAST, or WALL
CLADDING.

Engineering Hard, dense and extra strong

bricks which – in domestic work – are used chiefly for the walls of INSPECTION CHAMBERS and CESSPOOLS, and above ground for paving and external steps.

In old buildings, these bricks were often used as a DAMP-PROOF COURSE.

Facing Bricks that have excellent weathering properties and are used chiefly for their decorative appearance.

Glazed Also known as enamelled bricks, they have one long and one short face factory-fired with a white or coloured glazed finish.

They are very expensive.

Keyed A specially made brick with shallow, dovetailed grooves moulded in one long end and one short side of a brick to provide a key for plastering internal walls, or ROUGHCAST, RENDERING, or similar coverings on outside wall surfaces.

Rubber (or *Rubbed-brick*) A relatively soft textured brick that can be shaped by rubbing one brick against another or be carved with a chisel. An expensive brick, it is used chiefly for restoration work.

Rustic A brick with a mechanically finished texture as opposed to one having a natural finish – often given to bricks that would otherwise have a poor appearance.

Sand-faced A brick given a sand-finished surface and colouring during manufacture, either on one long face, or one long and one short face. These bricks must be handled with care for if chipped they will reveal their contrasting body colour.

Stocks Originally used to describe the yellow bricks made of river clay from the outskirts of London. Nowadays, stocks are often the stock or common brick used in a particular district.

Wire cuts Bricks that have been cut with wires, rather than pressed during manufacture and are therefore without a FROG – the indentation on one of the broad faces of common bricks.

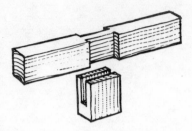

BRIDLE JOINT A form of MORTISE-AND-TENON JOINT, once used a great deal in traditional roofing but now more commonly found in modern furniture. The parts can be glued and screwed or glued and dowelled together to make a strong T- or angle joint.

BRITISH STANDARDS INSTITUTION (BSI) An independent organization financed jointly by its members and through the sale of its many publications. The Institution devises standards for manufacturers and distributors governing the quality, construction, dimensioning and testing of materials and products. It also draws up codes of practice, recommending and defining what is good practice in a particular trade or operation.

BRITISH THERMAL UNIT (BTU) The amount of heat required to raise the temperature of 1 lb of water by 1°F through 39°F to 40°F.

One BTU is a 100,000th part of a THERM.

BRUISING Dents caused in the surface of timber by hammer blows.

BRUSHES ◗ PAINT BRUSHES, WALL-PAPERING BRUSH

BTU ◗ BRITISH THERMAL UNITS

BUILDING BLOCKS Various types of hollow, solid or cellular blocks – larger than bricks – that are often used for the inner skin of CAVITY WALLS, or for internal walls.

Building blocks are made of various materials offering differing properties – some are made of dense concrete, suitable for LOAD-BEARING walls, others of lightweight concrete providing a high level of thermal insulation. Their lightness also makes them easier to handle on site.

Sizes vary but one common nominal size is 450 mm by 225 mm by 100 mm (18 ins. by 9 ins. by 4 ins.) thick.

BUILDING LINE An imaginary line, usually established by the local authorities, beyond which a building may not project. The line generally establishes the minimum distance allowed between the front of a property and the road it faces. On a corner site there are two building lines.

BUILDING PAPER A sandwich of bituminized fibre netting, laminated between sheets of tough brown paper. It is often used as a lining paper between a wall and WALL CLADDING, such as tiles or boarding, or beneath the tiles and BATTENS on a roof. In both cases it helps to keep out damp and draughts.

Building paper is unsuitable for a DAMP-PROOF COURSE.

Qualities and thicknesses of paper vary, and it is sold in several lengths and widths from 900 mm to 1830 mm (3 ft to 6 ft).

BUILDING REGULATIONS Legal requirements, framed under the powers of the Public Health Act and administered by local authorities, which are designed to ensure that most building or alteration work conforms to a set of minimum standards.

The regulations cover such subjects as structural work, as well as sanitation, ventilation, insulation, fire protection and heating installations.

The regulations apply to England and Wales, except for Inner London which has its own London Building Acts. Scotland and Northern Ireland, respectively, have their own Building Regulations.

Failure to comply with the regulations can mean having to pull the work down or alter it, or be fined a maximum of £100.
(◆ PLANNING PERMISSION)

BULLNOSE BRICK ◆ BRICKS
BULL NOSE PLANE ◆ PLANES
BUTT HINGE ◆ HINGES
BUTT JOINT A joint between adjacent pieces of wood that fit together square and flush.

C

CABINET SCRAPER A flat, rectangular piece of steel, about 0.8 mm thick and 115 mm by 75 mm (4½ ins. by 3 ins.) wide, with two cutting edges, used for finishing wood surfaces. Often used to give a clean, smooth finish to veneers where glasspaper would clog the grain with dust.

CABINET SCREWDRIVER ♦ SCREWDRIVERS

CABLE The copper conductors, or wires, that distribute electricity in a house, from the MAINS supply to the various outlet points, such as the SOCKET OUTLETS, SWITCHES and CEILING ROSES.

Cable is part of the permanent wiring in a house and should not be confused with FLEX, which has an entirely different function.

Cable is round or oval in cross section and normally has an outer covering of plastic (PVC). Older houses may still have cable encased in 'trs' (tough rubber sheathing) and, on rare occasions, lead.

The cable may be single core (one wire), twin core, twin core and an earth, or three core and an earth. The colours on the insulated wires are red for the live wire, black for neutral, and – when insulated – green for the earth. (Note: the new COLOUR CODING introduced in July 1970 does not apply to cable.)

Cables are made in various sizes with different current ratings. Three in common use are: 12 AMPS, 15 AMPS and 21 AMPS – 1.0 mm², 1.5 mm² and 2.5 mm², respectively.

(♦ COLOUR CODING; FLEX)

22

CALIPERS A steel, compass-like tool used for transferring the diameter or width of an object to a measuring rule.

Outside calipers have bowlegs, inside calipers have outward turned legs: both types made with or without a spring-controlled joint for making fine adjustments.

CALORIFIER ▶ HOT WATER CYLINDER

CAMES The metal strips used to secure the small panes of glass in LEADED LIGHTS (windows).

CAPE CHISEL ▶ CHISELS

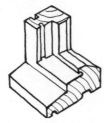

CAPILLARY GROOVE The elastic property of water can bridge a hair's breadth gap between two adjacent surfaces and cause moisture to rise above its own natural level – a characteristic known as capillary action.

The grooves in the sides of a window or door frame prevent this movement of moisture, and thereby stop dampness getting through to the inner walls.

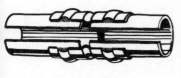

CAPILLARY JOINT A lightweight fitting used to make neat joints between lengths of copper or stainless steel tubing. There are two kinds of capillary joint: the integral ring fitting and the end-feed fitting.

The integral ring fitting consists of a short length of pipe, which is fractionally larger than the pipes to be joined and has a raised sleeve near each end; each sleeve contains a ring of solder. When the ends of the pipes are pushed together and the joint is heated with a BLOW-LAMP, the solder melts and spreads – due to capillary action. When it dries it forms a tightly-sealed joint.

An end-feed fitting does not have solder integrated, and must therefore be applied separately.

CAPPING Any material used to protect or give a decorative finish to the top of a fence or wall.

CARBORUNDUM A compound of carbon and silicon, second in hardness to diamond. Carborundum is used in various ways: as grit on certain abrasive papers; in powder form for levelling an OILSTONE; and as an oilstone for sharpening tools.

CARPETS There are three main types of carpet construction: woven, tufted and bonded.

Woven This is the traditional method used for the best quality carpet, where the backing material and the pile are woven together at the same time. Two typical types of woven carpet are Axminster and Wilton – not brand names but carpet types produced on the same kind of loom.

Tufted Non-woven carpets where the pile is stitched into a backing material and anchored with an adhesive. The pile may have cut or looped ends. Tufted carpets may have a second backing material of foam rubber to act as an underlay, i.e. an extra cushioning material.

Bonded These are available in a number of different finishes – the fibres bonded to an adhesive-coated backing material or needled into a backing until they are matted together.

Most fibres used for carpets are natural fibres, such as cotton, wool, hair, jute, rush and sisal; and synthetic fibres such as acrylic, nylon, polyester and polypropylene.

Many carpets are made from a blend of natural and synthetic fibres in order to gain the advantages of each, e.g. a wool/nylon carpet which has the high resilience of the wool combining with the hard-wearing characteristics of nylon.

Sizes are complicated, since carpets are made in strips, varying from 460 mm to 910 mm (18 ins. to 36 ins.) wide; broadloom, from 1830 mm to 5490 mm (6 ft to 18 ft); and squares, usually 3660 mm (12 ft) square or 2750 mm by 3660 mm (9 ft by 12 ft).

(◆ CARPET TILES)

CARPET TILES Squares of floor covering, made in various backing materials such as needlefelt and foam rubber, and with a range of different wear surfaces, such as woven, bonded or tufted materials.

Carpet tiles are easy for the amateur to lay and have the added convenience of being inter-changeable to minimize patches of excessive wear. The tiles may be laid loose, have a self-adhesive backing or be fixed to the floor with adhesive.

Popular sizes are 400 mm and 500 mm (roughly 16 in. and 20 in.) squares.

(◆ CARPETS)

CARRIAGE PIECE A strengthening timber on the underside of a staircase helping to support the TREADS and RISERS.

(◆ STRING)

CARTRIDGE FUSE ◆ FUSES

CASEMENT A window having one or more opening frames, i.e. hinged or pivoted sections, within an overall fixed framework of metal, hardwood or softwood.

CASTORS Ball- or wheel-shaped fittings that can be attached to the bottom of furniture legs. Castors simplify moving heavy pieces of furniture.

(◆ GLIDES)

CATSLIDE ROOF A sloping roof that extends from the main part of the roof to sweep down almost to ground level.

CAULKING Weatherproofing the gaps between the edges of door and window frames and adjacent wall surfaces with a flexibie filling compound. Non-setting mastics, which harden only on the surface and leave a skin that can be painted, are

injected through the nozzle of a cylindrical pack or tube, or a caulking gun.
(♦ MASTICS)

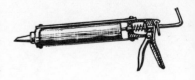

CAVITY INFILLING Improving the thermal value of a CAVITY WALL by filling the air space with insulation material – either a water repellent mineral wool, blown in under pressure, or a foamed plastic. This is injected under pressure through small holes drilled in the external walls, and solidifies to dry hard.

Both systems are proprietary methods that can be used on existing cavity walls.
(♦ MINERAL WOOL)

CAVITY WALL An external wall designed to keep out dampness and improve thermal insulation by incorporating a 50 mm (2 in.) cavity between two leaves of brick/block work. The inner leaf, which carries the loads of floors and the roof, is often constructed in load-bearing concrete BUILDING BLOCKS, for their high insulation value; the outer leaf may be in facing brick or stonework. Both leaves are linked by WALL TIES to give the wall additional stability.

The cavity is sealed around the edges of all door and window openings with a DAMP-PROOF COURSE separating the leaves, to prevent dampness passing from the outer to the inner walls.

The normal thickness of a cavity wall is 275 mm (11 ins.).
(♦ WALL TIES)

CEILING ROSE A decorative plate, usually made of wood, through which lighting FLEX hangs.

CEMENT A material that undergoes a chemical change and sets hard when mixed with water.

Cement is used to bind sand and other AGGREGATES together to make mortar and concrete.

CEMENT MORTAR ♦ MORTAR

CENTRAL HEATING (SPACE HEATING) A method of distributing heat – usually from a single source, such as a boiler – throughout a house. There are three basic systems in use: full central heating providing required temperatures to all living areas; partial central heating, providing heat to some but not all living areas; and background heating, providing lower temperatures to all living areas.

Systems can vary according to the type of fuel used, i.e. gas, oil, electricity or solid fuel.

The low pressure or gravity hot water system is the simplest. Water is heated in a boiler and circulates naturally through pipework, rising to the highest radiator and falling as it cools.

A small-bore heating system uses smaller pipes, usually 15 mm or 22 mm ($\frac{1}{2}$ in. or $\frac{3}{4}$ in.) in diameter, and has an electric CIRCULATION PUMP to force the water around the pipework and radiators.

A microbore (or minibore) system has even smaller pipes – 6 mm to 12 mm ($\frac{1}{4}$ in. to $\frac{7}{16}$ in.) in diameter – and also has a circulation pump.

Microbore is a relatively inconspicuous and easy system for the handyman to install; it is also quick to respond to its controls.

Other types of full, partial and background heating systems are:

Skirting heating A low-pressure hot water system, with a finned copper pipe inside a metal casing that is fixed around the perimeter of a room in place of a conventional SKIRTING. Heat escapes through a grille in the top of the casing.

Storage heating A system using large radiators, each of which contains a number of special heat-retaining blocks that are interlaced with an electric element; the blocks are encased in thick wraps of insulation material.

27

The blocks are heated by the element during the night, on an OFF-PEAK TARIFF, and release this heat by natural radiation throughout the following day to provide a high level of background warmth.

Some storage heaters have an integral fan that can push out the stored heat more quickly.

Heaters are made in various sizes and ratings, from 1½ kW to just under 4 kW, and need their own wiring circuits – they cannot be used on ordinary SOCKET OUTLETS.

Underfloor heating Electrically heated elements, or hot, water-filled pipes embedded in concrete floors to provide radiant heat. The floor acts in the same way as a storage heater and the heating is usually on an off-peak tariff.

Underfloor heating cannot be installed conveniently in an existing house.

Warm-air heating A system by which warm air – heated by a gas- or oil-fired boiler, or an electric storage heater – is fan-blown throughout a house by wood or metal ducting. The warm air emerges from grilles, fixed either in the floor or at low-level in dividing walls.

(♦ HEATERS)

CENTRE BIT ♦ BITS

CENTRING The timber framework used to support an arch while it is being built.

CENTRE PUNCH A steel tool, with an angled point, used with a hammer to mark accurate hole centres in metalwork.

Point diameters vary from 3 mm to 6 mm, with 100 mm to 175 mm (4 in. to 7 in.) long shafts.

CERAMIC TILES Glazed ceramic tiles suitable for surfacing walls, worktops and floors, are available in a wide range of colours (as well as white), patterns, textures and a few shapes, such as hexagonal.

Surface finishes may be matt, glazed or – in some cases – slip resistant.

The majority of tiles are 'field' tiles, which have small spacer lugs projecting on their edges that butt together and ensure that the joints on a tiled wall will be even throughout. When the joints are filled with GROUT the lugs are concealed.

Other types are the RE (round edge) tile, which has one rounded edge to provide a neat finish to a tiled area, and the REX (which has two rounded edges, adjacent to each other) used for corners. Neither the RE nor the REX has spacer lugs. A 'border' tile has square-cut edges with two of the edges glazed, and is used as an alternative to RE and REX tiles.

A range of ceramic tile sizes is produced but the two basic sizes in common use are: 108 mm by 108 mm by 4 mm ($4\frac{1}{4}$ ins. by $4\frac{1}{4}$ ins. by $\frac{5}{32}$ in.) thick, and 152 mm by 152 mm by 6 mm (6 ins. by 6 ins. by $\frac{1}{4}$ in.) thick.

Special heat-resistant tiles are also manufactured, 9 mm ($\frac{3}{8}$ in.) thick, suitable for tiled areas directly adjacent to cookers and fireplaces.

(♦ MOSAICS)

CESS-PIT ♦ CESSPOOL

CESSPOOL An underground brick, concrete or glass-fibre chamber used for the temporary storage of domestic sewage – chiefly in rural areas where there are no public sewers available.

Cesspools are emptied at regular pre-arranged intervals by local authorities who, in some cases, impose a charge.

The BUILDING REGULATIONS state that new cesspools must have a minimum capacity of 18 m³ (23.5 yds³) – about 4000 gallons.

A cesspool also describes a lead-lined box in the GUTTERS of some old houses, where water is emptied into a downpipe.

(♦ BOX GUTTER; SEPTIC TANK)

CHALK LINE Thin plastic or cotton line used by plasterers, floorlayers and bricklayers when setting out their work. The string is rubbed with a stick of chalk, stretched taut against the wall or floor surface, and plucked, transferring a sharply defined line to the surface.

Chalked string can be bought in a patent fitting, similar to a spring-loaded retractable rule, which chalks the line automatically as it is withdrawn.

CHAMFER The angled surface formed after an arris (corner) has been planed off at 45°.

A stopped chamfer splays off back to the arris.

CHANNEL A groove formed or cut in a concrete or asphalt surface to convey liquid from one area to another, such as rainwater to a drainage outlet. A channel in concrete may be lined with half-round stoneware pipes, laid IN SITU.

A channel is also the term for a steel beam.

(◗ ROLLED STEEL JOIST)

CHASE A groove cut in a brick, building block or concrete wall, or floor, to accommodate pipes or cables that are to be concealed beneath the surface with cement mortar or concrete.

CHIMNEY A brick or stone-built shaft, with a central flue that conveys smoke or fumes from an open fire or BOILER to the open air. The inside of the flue was traditionally lined with sand and cement to protect the brickwork.

Nowadays, chimneys are built with clay or terracotta liners to prevent condensation or the corrosive effects of gases damaging the brickwork.

If gas- or oil-fired central heating is installed in an old house, the existing flue is lined with a flexible aluminium tube, or a proprietary fluid is poured into the flue, around a temporary inflatable liner, to set hard.

CHIPBOARD Particles of softwood and waste timber, glued and bonded together under pressure to make a hard and stable sheet material. Edge-to-edge jointing of chipboard, however, needs reinforcing with blocks of softwood or proprietary plastic corner joints. The edges of chipboard also offer a poor grip for screws and should be lipped with softwood, e.g. when fitting hinges.

Common sizes available are 12 mm, 18 mm and 22 mm ($\frac{1}{2}$ in., $\frac{3}{4}$ in. and $\frac{7}{8}$ in.) thick and 2440 mm by 1220 mm (8 ft by 4 ft) wide.

Special flooring grade chipboard, with TONGUED-AND-GROOVED edges, can also be used as an excellent substitute for FLOOR BOARDS.

(◗ BLOCKBOARD; LAMINBOARD; PLYWOOD)

CHISELS (Metal) A variety of steel tools, a few of which are used for cutting metal, but most of which are for masonry work, ranging from rough-cutting tools to those used for the final shaping and smoothing of stone.

The most useful to the handyman are as follows:

Bolster A chisel with a broad cutting edge, used with a club hammer to cut bricks. Blades are 75 mm to 100 mm (3 ins. to 4 ins.) wide.

Cape Has a blunt, arrow-shaped head, used for cutting narrow grooves in stonework or metal. Particularly useful for chiselling out the mortar JOINTING between bricks.

Cold A heavy, general-purpose steel chisel that can be used for rough-cutting of metal, such as shearing off bolt or rivet heads.

A cold chisel is also used with a club hammer for cutting CHASES (grooves) in concrete, or chipping off waste material.

Lengths of shaft vary from 125 mm to 200 mm (about 5 ins. to 8 ins.), with 6 mm to 25 mm ($\frac{1}{4}$ in. to 1 in.) wide cutting edges.

CHISELS (Wood) Razor-sharp tools, with steel blades, used for making woodwork joints or cutting holes in wood. A variety of types and sizes of chisels are made – available with boxwood or hard plastic handles.

Common types in use are:

Firmer A strong, general-purpose chisel, with a stout blade that can be driven into wood with a mallet.

The steel blade is rectangular in cross section, about 100 mm (4 ins.) long, and available in cutting widths varying from 6 mm to 38 mm ($\frac{1}{4}$ in. to $1\frac{1}{2}$ ins.).

Bevelled edge Similar in many respects to a firmer chisel but with the long edges of the blade bevelled on the upper surface. This makes the chisel easier to use in awkward cutting areas or when undercutting, such as making a DOVETAILED JOINT.

The bevelled edge is wafer thin and easily chipped, and therefore the chisel should not be used with a mallet.

Available in similar sizes to firmer chisels.

Paring Can be either a firmer or bevelled edge chisel, but has a longer blade – about 175 mm (nearly 7 ins.).

A paring chisel is useful where the extra length is an advantage, e.g. when cutting a long groove.

Blade widths vary from 6 mm to 38 mm ($\frac{1}{4}$ in. to $1\frac{1}{2}$ ins.) long.

Mortise A strong-bladed chisel – almost square in cross section – used for cutting and clearing out narrow holes in woodwork, e.g. when making a MORTISE-AND-TENON JOINT.

Blades are 12 mm, 15 mm and 18 mm ($\frac{1}{2}$ in., $\frac{5}{8}$ in. and $\frac{3}{4}$ in.) wide, and the stocky beechwood handles can be struck safely with a mallet.

CHUCK ◗ DRILLS

CIRCUIT BREAKER ◗ FUSE

CIRCUIT FUSES ◗ FUSE

CIRCULAR SAW ◗ SAWS

CIRCULATION PUMP A small, electrically driven pump – sometimes referred to as an accelerator – used to force hot water through small-bore heating systems. (◗ CENTRAL HEATING)

CISTERN A cold water storage tank with an open top. Pipework distributes water to taps and appliances – including the hot water cylinder – throughout a house.

Cisterns are made in various materials, e.g. galvanized steel, polythene, asbestos-cement, and glass reinforced plastic (grp) – some rectangular, others round.

Sizes vary according to the requirements of local authorities, but for most average families, a 25 gallon actual capacity tank is suitable for cold water only; a 50 gallon tank is suitable for both hot and cold water supplies.

The actual capacity of a cistern is calculated to the level of the OVERFLOW PIPE – the NOMINAL SIZE if the cistern were filled to the rim.

(◗ COMBINATION TANK; HOT WATER CYLINDER)

CLADDING ◗ WALL CLADDING

CLAW HAMMER ◗ HAMMERS

CLAY TILES Floor tiles made from refined natural clays, fired at high temperatures, to produce tiles that are impervious to most fluids, easy to clean and similar in appearance to traditional QUARRY TILES.

Clay tiles are available in a variety of earthy reds, browns and yellows and in a range of sizes. Those in common use are 75 mm, 100 mm and 150 mm (3 ins., 4 ins. and 6 ins.) square, in thicknesses from 5 mm to 22 mm ($\frac{3}{16}$ in. to $\frac{7}{8}$ in.).

Surface finishes available are smooth,

grooved, ribbed or studded, and a few having a special non-slip finish.

Clay tiles have spacer lugs except for RE and REX specials. (♦ CERAMIC TILES).

CLEAR GLASS ♦ GLASS

CLENCH NAILING Driving a nail through a piece of wood and hammering the pointed end down flat.

CLOSED STRING ♦ STRING

CLOSER Part of a full BRICK used in brickwork to make the BOND. Two kinds are in common use: the king closer and the queen. Both can be bought as special standards, but in practice – especially on small jobs – are cut on site by bricklayers from full-size bricks.

CLOUT ♦ NAILS

CLUB HAMMER ♦ HAMMERS

COACH BOLT A round-headed bolt with a squared section of the shank beneath it. This fits into a corresponding shape cut in the woodwork so that the bolt will grip when tightened.

Suitable for a wide range of jobs, coach bolts are available in lengths up to 500 mm (about 20 ins.) and from 5 mm to 19 mm ($\frac{3}{16}$ in. to $\frac{3}{4}$ in.) diameter.

COACH SCREW A large screw with a square, bolt-like head that is driven into a pre-drilled hole with a spanner. Makes strong fixings in wood, e.g. fencing and partitioning.

Sizes from 25 mm to 406 mm (1 in. to 16 ins.) long and 6 mm to 25 mm ($\frac{1}{4}$ in. to 1 in.) in diameter.

CODES OF PRACTICE ♦ BRITISH STANDARDS INSTITUTION

COLD CHISEL ♦ CHISELS

COLD WATER STORAGE TANK ♦ CISTERN

COLOUR CODING Before July 1970, electric wiring was identified by the following colours of insulation: red for live, black for neutral, and green for earth.

This coding still applies to the CABLES

used for wiring a house. These colours will also be found on FLEXES attached to appliances bought before the above date.

All new appliances sold in Britain, however, must conform to the international colour coding system, with brown insulation for live wires, blue for neutral, and green and yellow for the earth.
(◆ FUSES)

COMBINATION SQUARE ◆ SQUARES

COMBINATION TANK This, as the name implies, is a proprietary prefabricated unit, containing hot and cold water storage tanks – one mounted above the other – within a single outer casing, or framework. It can easily be accommodated in a floor to ceiling cupboard and includes all the necessary plumbing pipework and fittings.

Although designed for small flats and bungalows, some combination cylinders and tanks, can service a whole house.

Made with both direct and indirect cylinders.
(◆ CISTERN; HOT WATER CYLINDER)

COMB JOINT ◆ BOX JOINT
COMMON BRICK ◆ BRICKS
COMPASS SAW ◆ SAWS
COMPRESSION JOINT A brass fitting used to joint copper pipework, or chromium-plated to joint stainless steel. There are two types of compression joint: the manipulative and the non-manipulative.

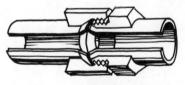

manipulative joint

The former demands an element of skill since the inside ends of the pipes to be joined must first be flared to fit over a tapered ring before the nuts are tightened. The non-manipulative joint is simpler: the ends of the pipes are cut square and united by a coupling nut.
(◆ CAPILLARY JOINT)

non-manipulative joint

CONCEALED HINGE ◆ HINGES

CONCRETE Sand, cement and aggregate mixed with water to form, when dry, a rock-hard homogeneous material.

The type of aggregate used and the proportions of the ingredients give concrete varying strengths according to its purpose – for drives, foundations, floors, lintels and so on.

A typical concrete mix is expressed as 1:2:4 – one part cement: two parts sand: four parts aggregate.

(◆ PRE-CAST CONCRETE; PRE-STRESSED CONCRETE; READY-MIXED CONCRETE; REINFORCED CONCRETE)

CONDENSATION The water droplets produced when warm, moist air, heavily laden with water vapour, comes into contact with a cold hard surface – a frequent cause of dampness in poorly ventilated rooms.

Condensation can usually be reduced with correct heating, ventilation and insulation.

(◆ PAINT, ANTI-CONDENSATION)

CONDUIT Metal or plastic tubing used to encase and protect CABLES from physical damage as well as the effects of dampness in a building.

Conduit is often buried beneath the surface of plaster in CHASES cut in brickwork or concrete.

CONSERVATION AREAS Areas designated by local planning authorities as being of special architectural or historic interest – having a character which is considered desirable to preserve or enhance.

In such areas Historic Building Grants may be available.

(◆ GRANTS)

CONSUMERS UNIT ◆ FUSE BOARD

CONTACT ADHESIVE ◆ ADHESIVES

CONTINUOUS HINGE ◆ HINGES

CONTRACT The agreement made and signed between a builder and the client, i.e. the employer. the document specifies the contract sum, the commencement and completion dates of the contractor's work, the cost of the work, the fees to be paid, and any other important details regarding the management of the work.

The contract documents usually include a set of WORKING DRAWINGS, a SPECIFI-CATION and sometimes a BILL OF QUANTITIES.

CONVECTOR HEATER ▶ HEATERS

COPING A brick, stone or tiled projection, or finish, to the top of a wall to protect it from the effects of weathering.

A coping stone that slopes away and down from the centreline, and overhangs the wall below, is a saddleback.

COPING SAW ▶ SAWS

CORBELLING One or more courses of brickwork that are built to overhang the courses below, in order to provide a larger bearing surface for a beam or roof truss.

Alternatively, corbelling may be used solely for decorative purposes.

For structural safety a wall should not be corbelled out more than one third the thickness of the wall below.

Also known as oversailing.

CORD SWITCH ▶ SWITCHES

CORK PAPER ▶ WALLPAPERS

CORK TILES An ideal floor covering where a warm, resilient and hard-wearing material is wanted, for example in a bathroom, kitchen or playroom.

Tiles are manufactured in three shades: light, medium and dark, with a plain sanded finish so that the tiles can be sealed after they have been laid in position. Alternative types have a pre-waxed finish, or a bonded, factory vinyl seal that makes them easy to keep clean.

The popular size is 305 mm (12 ins.) square and 3 mm and 5 mm ($\frac{1}{8}$ in. and $\frac{3}{16}$ in.) thick respectively, but others up to 457 mm (18 ins.) long are also made.

Less densely compressed cork tiles with large granules are suitable for wall coverings and pin-up boards.

CORNER TABLE PLATE A proprietary fitting used to make right-angled corner joints, such as the joint between two horizontal rails and a table leg.

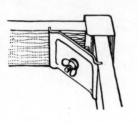

A screw-threaded bolt is fitted into the corner post. A metal plate is then slipped over the bolt and braced against the corner by tightening a wing nut.

Large brackets are 38 mm (1½ ins.) deep; small brackets 19 mm (¾ in.).

CORNICE A plain or ornamental timber or fibrous plaster casting, used to cover the angle between the walls and ceiling.

Also a moulded projection, usually cut in stone or carved in brick, at the top of an outside wall, to prevent weather-staining the surface below.

CORRUGATED FASTENER A piece of corrugated steel, with a sharpened edge, used for strengthening a BUTT JOINT between two pieces of timber, where appearance is of secondary importance.

COUNTERSINK BIT ▶ BITS

COUNTERSUNK SCREW ▶ SCREWS

COURSE A horizontal layer of bricks, plus the thickness of one horizontal mortar joint.

COVING A modern form of cornice – half round in cross section – used to conceal the angle between ceiling and walls and to disguise the hairline cracks which often develop in the corner.

Three different types of proprietary coving are made: Anaglypta; gypsum plaster; and polystyrene. All are fixed with adhesive recommended by the manufacturers.

COWL A clay or metal louvre that can be fixed to a chimney pot to improve down draught to an open fire.

CRAMPS Metal tools, many of which have screwed mechanisms for fine adjustments, used to grip or clamp workpieces together while glueing.

Bar or sash cramp A flat, steel bar with a screw adjustment at one end, and an adjustable peg that can be fitted into any one of a series of holes drilled in the bar. Bar lengths vary from 600 mm to 1500 mm (about 23½ ins. to 59 ins.).

Bar cramps are particularly useful for clamping large boards or window frames together.

G-cramp The G-shaped frame is made of aluminium, malleable iron or steel, and the 'tail' of the G is a screwed thread with a tommy bar or a wing nut. A G cramp is a versatile tool, useful as an 'extra hand' when holding a workpiece steady.

Sizes of the cramp's jaws when open vary from 20 mm to 300 mm (¾ in. to 12 ins.).

Mitre cramp A cramping tool that simplifies the accurate cutting and assembling of a MITRED JOINT. The tool can clamp wood that is between 50 mm and 115 mm (2 ins. and 4½ ins.) thick.

CRANKED HINGE ◗ HINGES

CRANKED STAY A folding bracket that has two metal arms, hinged and cranked at the middle. Suitable for a lightweight drop flap, such as a small cupboard front, the stay clicks into place when horizontal to provide a firm support, and 'breaks' when lifted slightly, allowing the front to fold up.

CRAZY PAVING Flat, broken slabs of natural stone or concrete, which are bedded together on sand or compacted soil, and pointed with mortar to form a paved surface, e.g. a path or terrace.

(◗ POINTING)

CREASING COURSE A double row of plain roofing tiles, used below a brick-on-edge capping, as part of the COPING to a wall.

CREOSOTE A liquid preservative suitable for timber, made from coal and wood-tar. Creosote can be brushed on to timber but is more effective if it is steeped alternately in hot and cold solutions. Pressure impregnation – a factory process – is far more effective.

An oily brown liquid, with a strong smell, creosote cannot easily be covered with paint.

CRESCENT SPANNER ⧫ SPANNERS

CREVICE BRUSH ⧫ PAINT BRUSHES

CROSS-CUT SAW ⧫ SAWS

CROSS-GRAIN Timber which does not have the grain running in a pronounced direction, owing to the way it was cut from the tree.

Cross-grain timber is difficult to saw or work with.

CROSS-PEIN HAMMER ⧫ HAMMERS

CROW BAR A 29 mm (about 1⅛ in.) diameter steel bar, 1.5 m (5 ft) long, used for levering heavy weights, or similar jobs. The bar has a chisel shape at one end and a point at the other.

CUPS AND SCREWS ⧫ SCREW CUPS and WASHERS

CUT STRING ⧫ STRINGS

CUTTING GAUGE ⧫ GAUGES

CUTTING-IN BRUSH ⧫ PAINT describing the technique of painting a straight or curved line against the edge of another painted surface.

CUTTING-IN BRUSH ⧫ PAINT BRUSHES

CYLINDER ⧫ HOT WATER CYLINDER

CYLINDER NIGHT LATCH ⧫ LOCKS AND LATCHES

D

DADO The lower half of a wall, usually defined by a timber moulding, either panelled in wood or covered with an embossed paper.

DAMP-PROOF COURSE (d.p.c.) A layer of impervious material that is built into certain parts of a building to prevent damp affecting the interior. See left.

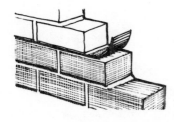

A d.p.c. in walls that are directly in contact with the ground is usually 150 mm (6 ins.) above soil level. Other typical places for d.p.c.s are beneath COPING stones and window sills; in CHIMNEY stacks and around door and window openings in CAVITY WALLS.

Rigid materials, such as slate, were once common, but are rarely used nowadays since they can crack with settlement and render a d.p.c. useless. Instead, flexible materials, such as bituminized hessian, or thin lead sheet sandwiched between layers of bituminous felt, are used.

Proprietary systems of combating RISING DAMP include injecting silicon fluid into the affected part of the wall. The fluid congeals and dries to form an impenetrable barrier. Other systems include methods of ventilation and drainage, and electro-osmosis – eliminating the electric charge in the earth and wall that assists moisture to rise.

DAMP-PROOF MEMBRANE A layer of waterproof material that is incorporated in the construction of a ground floor to ensure the internal floor finish remains dry and sound. A damp-proof membrane is

always linked to d.p.c.s in walls to ensure continuity of damp proofing.
(◆ DAMP-PROOF COURSE)

DATUM A point on site that has been established with a level base and given a value to which all other levels can be related during building work.

Datum is generally fixed at a specific height, such as the finished ground floor level, so that all other levels can then be measured conveniently, up or down from Datum, when setting out a building.

DAYLIGHT SIZE ◆ SIGHT SIZE

DEAD LEG The length of pipe from a HOT WATER CYLINDER to its draw-off points, i.e. taps.

Water cools in the pipe when it is not being used and a time lag occurs between a tap being opened and hot water arriving.

Some local authorities specify the maximum dead leg allowed in order to minimize the waste of heat.

DEAD LOCK ◆ LOCKS AND LATCHES

DEATH-WATCH BEETLE ◆ WOODWORM

DIE NUT A steel nut used to clean or re-cut an existing screw thread, e.g. a damaged or rusty thread on a bolt.

DIMMER SWITCH ◆ SWITCHES

DIRECT CYLINDER ◆ HOT WATER CYLINDER

DISC SANDER ◆ POWER TOOL ATTACHMENTS

DISTRIBUTION FUSEBOARD ◆ FUSE BOARD

DOG-LEG STAIR A staircase with two flights, and a half landing between them.

DOME-HEADED SCREW ◆ SCREWS

DOOR FRAME A rebated wooden surround to which a door is hinged. Stronger than a DOOR LINING, a frame is generally used for external door openings or, internally, where heavy solid doors are to be hung.

DOOR FURNITURE The collective term describing hinges, locks, handles, levers, knobs, fingerplates, letter boxes and other similar fittings used in house building.

DOOR LINING A wooden surround to an internal door opening, to which a door is hinged.

(◆ DOOR FRAME; DOOR STOP)

DOORS A wide range of standard types and sizes of doors is manufactured; they are usually identified by the construction, e.g. solid, flush, panelled, ledged-and-braced, louvred, and glazed.

Doors also vary in their thickness – a critical factor in cases where doors must have a fire resistance rating of, say, half an hour or an hour, in order to satisfy a local authority's requirements.

DOOR STOP The rebated edge of a door frame, or the planted strips of timber nailed to a DOOR LINING, which the door closes against.

(◆ DOOR FRAME)

DORMER A window that projects from a pitched roof and has a flat or pitched roof of its own.

DOUBLE GLAZING Windows with two layers of glass and an air space between them to provide thermal or acoustic insulation. The space may be as little as 6 mm ($\frac{1}{4}$ in.) for maximum thermal insulating properties, or not less than 50 mm (2 ins.) for minimum sound insulation.

Various proprietary systems are manufactured and double glazing can be made up by the handyman.

DOUBLE-HUNG SASH A window consisting of two SASHES, i.e. glazed windows that slide up and down within a fixed frame. Each sash is counterbalanced by two weights, attached to sash cords and suspended in vertical hollows within the sides of the window frame.

Some types of sash window have spring balances instead of weights.

DOVETAIL JOINT A strong corner joint used in making good quality traditional joinery.

A secret dovetail has the dovetails hidden – with only the meeting corners of the mitred edges showing.

DOVETAIL NAILING ◗ SKEW NAILING

DOVETAIL SAW ◗ SAWS

DOWELS Short, cylindrical pieces of hardwood, used for making strong, glued joints in woodwork. Ready-cut dowels, of varying diameters can be bought from DIY shops in small packs. Strips of dowelling rod for cutting to length as required, can be bought from both DIY shops and builders' merchants.

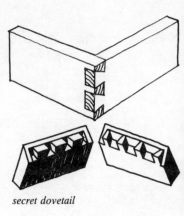

secret dovetail

DOWNPIPE ◗ GUTTERS AND DOWNPIPES

DPC ◗ DAMP-PROOF COURSE

DRAINCOCK A tap at the lowest point of a tank or water system which can be opened to drain the contents.

DRAIN PLUG A plug or stopper that can be fitted into an underground drainage pipe, where it joins an INSPECTION CHAMBER, to form a watertight seal when testing drains.

DRAIN RODS Cane rods that can be screwed together and fitted with interchangeable heads, for clearing blockages in underground drainage pipes.

A set of drain rods can often be hired from builders' merchants and usually contains a rubber plunger, or a corkscrew head – both of which will generally clear most blockages.

DRAINS The method by which sewage and, in most cases, rainwater is conveyed from a house to the main (public) sewer.

DRAUGHT EXCLUDERS Proprietary fittings that can be attached to door and window openings to reduce or eliminate draughts.

Excluders may be metal or plastic strips, expanded foam padding with a self-adhesive face, or fibre or rubber strips fixed with adhesive or non-ferrous nails.

DRILL-BIT SHARPENER An electric appliance, with a grinding wheel inside it, which simplifies sharpening drill BITS.

Suitable for sharpening bits from 3 mm to 9 mm ($\frac{1}{8}$ in. to $\frac{3}{8}$ in.).

DRILLS Tools that can be fitted with different types of cutting heads (BITS) for boring holes in wood, metal or plastic. Those commonly used by the handyman are:

Brace A cranked tool used to bore larger holes in wood than can be made with a hand drill or power drill. The brace can be fitted with special BITS, including countersink and screwdriver bits.

The more sophisticated type of brace has a ratchet mechanism that enables the tool to be used in a confined space where a full turn of the handle would be impossible.

The popular size of brace is 250 mm (10 ins.) – the diameter (or sweep) of the circle, travelled by one turn of the handle.

Breast A larger version of the hand drill which has an extension with a curved breast plate; the user can lean against this to increase pressure when drilling. Most have two gear ratios for drilling at different speeds.

A breast drill is especially useful when drilling into metal or masonry, but is also used for drilling into wood.

Sizes from 275 mm to 450 mm (roughly 10$\frac{3}{4}$ ins. to 17$\frac{3}{4}$ ins.) long, for drilling holes up to 12 mm ($\frac{1}{2}$ in.) diameter.

Hand drill (wheelbrace) Used with twist drill bits for holes up to 8 mm ($\frac{5}{16}$ in.) diameter, in wood or metal.

The tool has a toothed gear wheel that facilitates turning the drive handle at two different speeds; a side, steadying handle; and a chuck (bit holder), which usually has three self-centring jaws that grip the bit.

Most hand drills have exposed gear wheels, but modern models have the gears enclosed in a metal casing to protect them.

Lengths from 230 mm to 325 mm (roughly 9 ins. to 12½ ins.).

Power drill A versatile and invaluable electric tool, that can be used – with the appropriate attachments – for drilling, grinding, buffing, sanding, polishing, and such jobs as stirring paint.

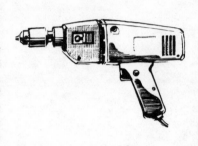

There are many types and sizes of power drill manufactured, for a range of varied purposes; but for most domestic jobs the two-speed drill is a worthwhile buy: it makes one speed turns up to 900 revolutions per minute, and the other up to 2500/3000 rpm. The gear change is usually made by flicking a small switch.

Different speeds and twist bit sizes are necessary when drilling into different materials. The recommended speeds for the following sizes and materials are:
Wood: up to 10 mm (⅜ in.) diameter – 2500/3000 rpm; from 10 mm to 25 mm (⅜ in. to 1 in.), a maximum of 1000 rpm.
Steel: up to 6.5 mm (¼ in.) diameter – 2500/3000 rpm; from 6.5 mm to 10 mm (¼ in. to ⅜ in.) a maximum of 1000 rpm.
Other metals, masonry and glass: up to 1000 rpm.
(◗ POWER-DRILL ATTACHMENTS)
Push drill A small hand tool for drilling 2 mm to 17 mm (¹⁄₁₆ in. to ¹¹⁄₁₆ in.) diameter holes in wood and plastic. As pressure is applied to the handle the drill bit revolves.

DROP PATTERN A decorative design or motif on wallpapers or vinyl wall-coverings that is repeated diagonally across the width of the material. Alternate motifs line through horizontally when correctly hung.
(◗ SEMI-PLAIN; SET PATTERN)

DRUM SANDER ◗ SANDING
MACHINES

DRY ROT A serious form of decay in timber caused by a fungus – usually *merulius lacrymans* – attacking damp wood in poorly ventilated conditions.

Dry rots spreads rapidly and easily and should be eradicated with specialist advice. (◗ WET ROT)

DUCTING A continuous cavity formed in the structure of a building to accommodate CABLES or service pipes passing from one floor to another.

In a warm air central heating system, metal ducting is used to convey the air from the heat source to the outlet grilles.

DWARF WALL A low wall, usually built in brick, that either supports the JOISTS beneath a SUSPENDED FLOOR, or is used for garden walling.

E

EARTH CONDUCTOR A connection that links part of the main CABLE with the earth (or subsoil) by means of a metal plate or rods to provide a return path for electric current.

EASEMENTS Certain rights that one owner has over another owner's land, e.g. the right of light for a window that overlooks a neighbour's land.

EDGE LIPPING Strips of softwood or hardwood glued and pinned to the edge of BLOCKBOARD or PLYWOOD to provide a finished appearance as well as, perhaps, a better material for fixing hinges etc.

EFFLORESCENCE A white powdery substance that sometimes appears on the surface of newly completed brickwork. Caused by soluble salts in the bricks and mortar crystallizing as moisture evaporates, it is an unattractive but harmless stain that eventually disappears.

EGGSHELL Paint that dries with a semi-gloss finish.

ELBOW An angled pipe fitting that enables two lengths of pipe to be connected to each other.

ELECTRIC DRILL ♦ DRILLS

ELECTRIC PAINT-STRIPPER An electric tool that heats and thereby softens paintwork so that it is more easily removed from wood or metal.

Power rating: 600 to 700 WATTS.

ELECTRICIAN'S PLIERS ♦ PLIERS

ELECTRICIAN'S SCREWDRIVER ♦ SCREWDRIVERS

ELECTROLYTIC ACTION When plumbing pipes and fittings of dissimilar

metals are used in conjunction with each other, galvanic action can cause one of the metals to corrode at the expense of the other. For example, HARD WATER passing through copper pipes will dissolve minute particles of copper, depositing them on the surface of a galvanized steel tank and thereby accelerating its corrosion.
(♦ SACRIFICIAL ANODE)

EMBOSSED PAPER ♦ WALLPAPERS
EMERY CLOTH ♦ ABRASIVES
EMULSION PAINT ♦ PAINT
END GRAIN The exposed surface of timber that is cut across the grain.
END-TO-END-JOINTS Methods of lengthening timber by joining it end to end. Three suitable joints are:

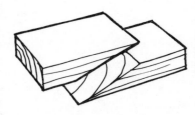

Lapped One piece of timber is lapped over the end of the other – the length of the lap three times the maximum thickness of the wood – and bolted together. A TIMBER CONNECTOR may also be used to strengthen the shear strength of the joint.
Reinforced butt The timbers are BUTT-JOINTED together and fitted with plywood plates or 'splints' glued and screwed to the sides.

The length of the plates is four times the maximum thickness of the wood.
Scarf The two ends of the timbers to be joined are splayed, glued and – where extra strength is needed – bolted together with FISH PLATES. The length of the splay is six times the maximum thickness of the wood.

ENGINEERING BRICK ♦ BRICKS
ENGINEER'S HAMMER ♦ HAMMERS
ENGLISH BOND ♦ BONDS
EPOXY RESIN ♦ ADHESIVES

ESCUTCHEON The protective and sometimes ornamental plate – made of metal or plastic – that surrounds a keyhole.
EXPANDED METAL Sheet metal that has been perforated with staggered rows of

small slits and then drawn apart, to form a mesh.

Expanded metal is sometimes used as a backing material, instead of plasterboard, when surfacing a STUD (wooden) partition wall or a ceiling with plaster. It can also be used when cement RENDERING the outer surface of a building and for reinforcing brick/concrete blockwork.

EXPANSION JOINT A flexible joint that allows adjacent parts of a building or fitting to expand and contract naturally, with moisture and temperature changes, without damaging the structure. Expansion joints are used in pipework and roof coverings, and brick and blockwork walls over a certain length.

EXPANSION TANK ◆ HOT WATER CYLINDER

EXPANSIVE BIT ◆ BITS

EXPANDED POLYSTYRENE ◆ INSULATING MATERIALS

EXTENDING LADDER A timber or aluminium ladder, with two or three sections, which can be telescoped or extended to an average maximum of 15.3 m (16.66 yds).

EXTENSION CABLE A length of CABLE that enables a power-driven tool, such as an electric drill, to be used in a place remote from a power source.

Extension cables can be bought in standard lengths from 8 m to 100 m (25 ft to 300 ft).

EXTRACTOR FAN An electric fan that can be fitted into the thickness of an external wall or a window pane, in order to extract steam, smoke or odours from a room – generally a kitchen or bathroom.

An extractor fan is usually necessary for any internal lavatory that does not have natural ventilation, i.e. a window. The fan is fitted in an external wall and linked to the compartment by metal trunking or ducting.

EYEBROW WINDOW A window, in a sloping roof, that is gently curved at the top to resemble a shallow segment. Sometimes referred to as an eyebrow dormer.

F

FACING BRICK ♦ BRICKS

FAIENCE Terracotta (i.e. once-fired clay) tiles, with an impervious glazed finish – either transparent or coloured.

FAIRFACED BRICK Brickwork that is laid with facing bricks and mortar joints neat enough to present a finished decorative surface.
(♦ BRICKS)

FAN CONVECTOR ♦ HEATERS

FASCIA The softwood board, attached to the foot of the RAFTERS on a sloping roof, the ends of the JOISTS on a flat roof, to which the guttering is fixed.
(♦ GUTTERS AND DOWNPIPES)

FEED-AND-EXPANSION TANK ♦
HOT WATER CYLINDER

FEELER GAUGE A tool with a set of thin steel blades, each of a different thickness, used to measure minutely small gaps, such as that between electric contact-breaker points.

Each blade is marked with its thickness – a typical gauge has ten blades and measures from 0.001 mm.

FIBRE BUILDING BOARD A sheet material made from wood or vegetable fibres compressed during manufacture to make strong and dense HARDBOARD, or left in its unpressed state to be used as insulating board.

FIBRE PLUG ♦ WALL PLUGS

FILLERS Materials used for filling holes and cracks in plaster or woodwork.
(♦ STOPPING)

FILES Steel cutting tools for smoothing the rough edges of metal or wood.

There are a great many types of file made to suit a variety of different jobs, and with many variations of cutting surfaces.

Files are classified by the way the teeth are arranged on the blade: usually, the more the teeth the smoother the cut, and the longer the file the coarser it is.

Teeth arrangements are known as single cut, double cut, and curved tooth. Single cut files have teeth arranged in single diagonal rows across the blade; a double cut has a second diagonal row, criss-crossing the first at an angle of 40°.

Four types are useful for most general purpose jobs: flat, round, half round and triangular. Sizes from 100 mm to 450 mm (4 ins. to 18 ins.) long.

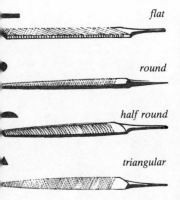

flat

round

half round

triangular

FILLET A thin strip of wood, often triangular in cross-section, used for packing out the corner junction between a flat roof and a wall. Also describes the wood fixed to a FASCIA on a flat roof, which prevents water running over the edge.

FILLING KNIFE A tool with a flexible steel blade, used for filling cracks in wood or plaster.

Blade widths vary from 25 mm to 100 mm (1 in. to 4 ins.).

FINGER JOINT ▶ BOX JOINT
FIRMER CHISEL ▶ CHISELS
FIRMER GOUGE ▶ GOUGES

FIRRINGS Triangular or sloping pieces of SOFTWOOD, nailed to the tops of JOISTS on a flat roof in order to ensure the finished surface, such as boarding and felt, has sufficient slope to shed rainwater.

FISH PLATES Pieces of wood or sheets of metal used to strengthen LENGTH-ENING JOINTS, that is lengths of timber joined end to end. The fish plates are secured through the timbers with bolts.

FIXED LIGHT A window which is made not to open, unlike an OPENING LIGHT, SASH or CASEMENT.

FLAGSTONES Paving-size slabs of natural stone, or pavings made from reconstructed stone.

FLASHINGS Strips of lead, zinc, copper or BITUMINIOUS FELT, used to waterproof external junctions in a building between different planes or materials. For example, a flashing would be used between a flat roof and an adjacent wall.

FLAT-NOSED PLIERS ◗ PLIERS

FLAUNCHING CEMENT MORTAR used to form a curved surface around the base of chimney pots on a chimney stack. Flaunching not only helps to secure the pots but also protects the top of the chimney's brickwork from excessive weathering.

FLEMISH BOND ◗ BONDS

FLETTON ◗ BRICKS

FLEX A flexible cord (i.e. a conductor of electricity) used to connect an appliance, such as a vacuum cleaner, to a SOCKET OUTLET, via a plug.

The conductors in both 2 core and 3 core flexes are individually sheathed in rubber or plastic insulators, and coupled together by another outer sheathing of thicker insulation material. Some 2 core flexes are twisted together without an outer sheath.

Unlike CABLE (which has one thick wire for each conductor), flex has a number of fine strands. The greater the number of strands, the thicker the flex and the greater its amperage rating.

All 3 core flexes on appliances bought since July 1970, when the new COLOUR CODING was introduced, have brown insulation on the live wire, blue on the neutral, and green and yellow on the earth.

Older appliances will have the old colours of red for live, black for neutral, and green for earth.

2 core flex is not governed by colour coding, since it is used only for lighting and non-earthed equipment.

Flexes are rated in amperes, relative to

the loads they will carry, and can be used as follows: 3 amp for lighting; 6 amp for low-rated appliances, such as a single bar heater; 10 amp for between 1000 and 2000 watts; and 15 amp for the more powerful appliances, such as a washing machine.

FLEXIBLE DRIVE ◗ POWER TOOL ATTACHMENTS

FLEXIBLE RULE ◗ RULES

FLEXIBLE VINYL ◗ PLASTIC FLOORING

FLOATS Wood or metal tools used to give a fine-textured or smooth finish, respectively, to concrete, cement or plaster work.

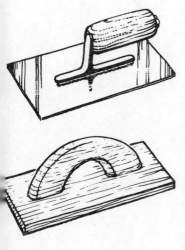

The steel float, also known as a flooring trowel, has a steel blade and may have square corners, or one end slightly pointed.

Metal floats are 350 mm to 450 mm (approximately 14 ins. to 18 ins.) long; wooden floats 125 mm by 275 mm (roughly 5 ins. by 11 ins.).

FLOCK PAPER ◗ WALLPAPER

FLOORBOARDS SOFTWOOD boards, generally 25 mm (1 in.) thick and 150 mm (6 ins.) wide, fixed to floor JOISTS with FLOORING BRADS. Most floorboards are square-edged and therefore BUTT-JOINTED, but TONGUED-AND-GROOVED boards make a stronger and draught-proof floor.

A flooring grade of tongued-and-grooved CHIPBOARD can be used in place of floorboards.

FLOOR COVERINGS ◗ CARPETS; CARPET TILES; CERAMIC TILES; CLAY TILES; CORK TILES; LINOLEUM; PLASTIC FLOORING; QUARRY TILES; WOOD BLOCK FLOORING

FLOORING BRAD ◗ NAILS

FLOORING SAW ◗ SAWS

FLOOR SANDERS ◗ SANDING MACHINES

FLOOR SEALERS ◗ SEALERS

FLOW PIPE The pipe conveying heated water from the BOILER to the HOT WATER CYLINDER.

FLUE ◗ CHIMNEY

FLUSH HINGE ◗ HINGES

FLUSH JOINT A joint where adjacent surfaces are flat.

FLUSHING VALVE A pressure-operated valve that releases a regulated amount of water to flush a water closet. The valve replaces the need for a conventional storage CISTERN, but is considered by some authorities to waste water and is not therefore permitted in all areas of the country.

FLUX A substance used in soldering that acts as a cleaning agent and helps heated metals to fuse together. Different fluxes are used for different metals, e.g. a phosphoric-based acid flux for stainless steel CAPILLARY JOINTS; a chloride-based flux for copper capillary joints; and a resin solder for electrical work. A resin-cored solder – combining both solder and flux – can be bought and is suitable for small electrical jobs.

FOAM ROLLER ◗ PAINT ROLLERS

FOLDING RULE ◗ RULES

FOLDING STAY ◗ FURNITURE STAYS

FOLDING WEDGES A pair of tapered wedges that slide against each other, in opposite directions, to force two surfaces apart – such as a bowed DOOR LINING and the adjacent wall.

FOUNDATION The concrete base beneath structural walls that spreads the loads evenly to prevent settlement cracks. The strength of a foundation is calculated according to the nature of the soil it rests upon which, with some soils, may mean that it is necessary to use REINFORCED CONCRETE.

The various types of foundation used for houses are:

Piles Primarily used on clay sites where

there is a risk of seasonal soil movement. Deep circular holes are bored with an auger and filled with reinforced concrete. A series of reinforced beams (horizontal strips of concrete) built on the tops of the piles provide a base for the house walls.

Slab (or *Raft*) A flat slab of concrete, which is usually reinforced, used on sites where normal strip foundations would be too expensive, e.g. on waterlogged soil or where firm subsoil is too deep.

Strip The most common types of all – a continuous length of concrete (sometimes reinforced) beneath all major structural walls.

FRAME SAW ◗ SAWS

FRENCH DOORS ◗ FRENCH WINDOWS

FRENCH POLISHING A traditional and skilled technique of giving natural or stained HARDWOOD a highly polished finish, by applying a coat of shellac dissolved in methylated spirit.

FRENCH WINDOWS A pair of glazed windows, with a centre meeting rail, that extend to floor level and serve as doors. Also known as French doors.

FRETSAW ◗ SAWS

FRICTION STAY ◗ FURNITURE STAY

FRIEZE Internally, the parts of a wall above a picture rail and beneath the ceiling.

FROG The indentation in some BRICKS that partly reduces their self-weight. A wall's strength is also said to be improved if bricks are laid frog upwards and filled with MORTAR.

FUNGICIDAL PAINT ◗ PAINTS

FURNITURE BEETLE ◗ WOODWORM

FURNITURE STAYS Metal or plastic fittings, used on cupboards, to support flaps that fold down to provide a level work surface. A pair of stays is used for each flap – one end of each stay fixed to the cupboard frame, the other to the flap.

There are several types of action, two of which are the friction stay and the folding stay. The first will hold the flap open in any position. Some types are spring-loaded to close with fingertip control.

The folding stay has an elbow joint

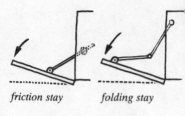

friction stay   *folding stay*

FUSE BOARD Circuit fuses are collected together and mounted on a board, or in one or more metal boxes, called the distribution board. This is usually positioned in the vicinity of the meters and the mains on/off switch.

A modern piece of equipment is the consumer unit – a box that contains all circuit fuses *and* the mains on/off switch.

Houses with OFF-PEAK STORAGE HEATING, have separate consumer units and meters.

FUSE A safety device in the form of a short length of thin wire that melts if too much current flows through it. This breaks the circuit and protects the main wiring, or any appliances, from being damaged by over-loading, due to a freak boost in public supplies, a short circuit, or too many appliances used for a circuit's rating.

Each circuit is protected by a main fuse, and every appliance wired to a 13 amp plug – one with three rectangular pins – is also protected by a fuse.

There are two types of fuse: the rewirable and the cartridge.

Rewirable A porcelain holder, with plug pins linked by fuse wire.

Cartridge A tube of porcelain or similar

incombustible material, with a copper cap at each end linked – through the centre of the tube – by fuse wire. The current carrying capacity of the wire is marked on the outside of the tube. When a cartridge fuse fails the whole is replaced – it cannot be rewired.

Fuse wire for repairing rewirable fuses is sold in three ratings (or thicknesses): 5 amp, 15 amp and 30 amp – the last being the thickest.

A lighting circuit has a 5 amp fuse, a ring circuit a 30 amp. Other circuits may have a 15 amp, 20 amp, and a 45 amp fuse – the last for an electric cooker.

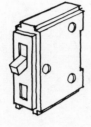

A more expensive but easier to use alternative to a conventional fuse is a miniature circuit breaker (MCB). This works as an automatic switch, cutting itself off when overloading occurs. To restore the supply instantly a button is pressed, or a switch thrown. Repeated cut-outs however, mean there is a fault within the circuit which must be put right.

G

GABLE The triangular area of an external wall, beneath the end of a PITCHED ROOF.

GALVANIZED METAL Iron or steel that has been coated with a layer of zinc to prevent corrosion. Galvanizing is an industrial process.
(♦ SHERARDIZED METAL)

GALVANIZED ROOFING NAIL ♦ NAILS

GARDEN WALL BOND ♦ BONDS

GARNET PAPER ♦ ABRASIVES

GATE VALVE A hand-operated on/off valve, which is used in plumbing to control the flow of water in a pipe.

GAUGED BRICKWORK Relatively soft bricks that have been sawn and rubbed to accurate shapes on site and laid with precision jointing – about 3 mm ($\frac{1}{8}$ in.) thick. Also known as 'rubbed' brickwork, it was often used for doors and window arches on late seventeenth- and early eighteenth-century houses.

GAUGE ROD ♦ STOREY ROD

GAUGES Tools used for marking or setting out accurate measurements in woodwork, chiefly when making joints.

There are two basic types: a marking gauge and a cutting gauge. Both are made of hardwood and have a 237 mm (roughly 9$\frac{1}{2}$ ins.) long shaft, with a stock that slides along it, secured with a thumb screw.

The marking gauge has a steel pin to score marked lines in the wood; the cutting gauge has a steel blade for use when scoring across the grain. Another version of the

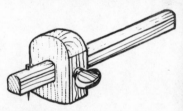
marking gauge

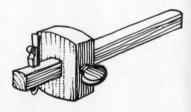
cutting gauge

mortise gauge

marking gauge is the mortise gauge. This has two steel pins, that can be moved to set distances apart, and is used to simplify setting out MORTISE-AND-TENON JOINTS.

GAUGING BOX A bottomless box, made to a predetermined size and used for simplifying the measurement of a SAND and AGGREGATE mixture, before CEMENT and water are added. The box is placed on the ground where the cement or concrete is to be mixed so save the necessity of carrying heavy loads.

G-CRAMPS ◗ CRAMPS

GENERAL IMPROVEMENT AREAS Districts, designated by local councils, that are in need of special attention in order to improve the environment – as well as properties – and make the neighbourhood more pleasant to live in.

In these areas councils have special powers to ensure that rented properties are improved. Higher rates of grants are also available to house owners.

(◗ GRANTS)

GENTS SAW ◗ SAWS

GEORGIAN-WIRED GLASS ◗ GLASS

GIMLET A handy tool for making small holes in wood, such as starting holes for screws or cup-hooks. The end of the steel shaft has a spiral screw thread.

Shaft diameters are 3 mm to 9 mm ($\frac{1}{8}$ in. to $\frac{3}{8}$ in.).

GLASS There are two main types in common use: sheet glass and float glass. Sheet glass – from 3 mm to 6 mm ($\frac{1}{8}$ in. to $\frac{1}{4}$ in.) thick – is the cheapest but, due to its method of manufacture, it is inclined to distort vision and be slightly reflective. It is therefore more suitable for garages, sheds and greenhouses.

Float glass – from 4 mm to 25 mm (roughly $\frac{1}{8}$ in. to 1 in.) thick – is completely transparent, having smooth polished sur-

61

faces, and is suitable for all windows, including double-glazed units. The thicker sizes are particularly useful for sound insulation.

Sheet glass 4 mm (about $\frac{1}{8}$ in.) thick, is the equivalent of the old 32 oz float glass – a pre-metrication term.

There are various other kinds of glass useful to the householder:

Antique An attractive glass of uneven thickness, with textured surfaces that resemble medieval glass. It is expensive but ideal for 'period' windows or small areas of decorative glass.

Armourplate A toughened glass with a high resistance to impact. If it does break, however, it disintegrates and crumbles into small pieces. It cannot be cut or drilled by the handyman.

Available in thickness varying from 5 mm to 19 mm ($\frac{3}{16}$ in. to $\frac{3}{4}$ in.) and in a range of manufactured sizes.

Glass blocks Translucent, non-load-bearing bricks, capable of carrying their own weight only, and therefore suitable for screen walls or panelled areas in external walls, e.g. beside a staircase landing.

Glass blocks can be laid like ordinary BRICKS but above certain lengths and areas they need reinforcing with intermediate supports. Manufacturers produce glass bricks in various sizes and patterns.

Translucent Glass that is suitable where privacy without loss of light is important, such as in a bathroom. It has one side of the glass polished smooth and the other patterned or textured: the more textured the surface the greater the degree of obscurity.

Two standard thicknesses are available: 3 mm and 5 mm ($\frac{1}{8}$ in. and $\frac{3}{16}$ in.) in a range of twenty-nine different patterns.

Wired (Georgian) Glass that is reinforced with 13 mm ($\frac{1}{2}$ in.) square or diamond-shaped mesh of steel wire. It is suitable for carport roofs or similar places where, if broken, the glass will not scatter dangerous shards.

It is 6 mm (¼ in.) thick, and available with a transparent (polished) or translucent (roughcast) finish.

Wired glass should be bought cut to size, since it is difficult for the amateur to handle.

GLASS BRICKS ◆ GLASS

GLASS CUTTER A tool with a hardened steel wheel, or a fragment of industrial diamond, used for cutting glass. The best type has replaceable wheels.

GLASS FIBRE MATERIALS A synthetic material consisting of minute filaments of glass impregnated with resins. It is used to make tough, corrosion-resistant items, such as corrugated sheeting, or as a filler for insulation quilting.

(◆ INSULATION MATERIALS)

GLASS SLATE A pane of glass that is cut to the same size as a slate and fitted in the same way to TILING BATTENS on a roof, to admit natural light to attic or roof space.

GLAZED BRICK ◆ BRICKS

GLAZING BARS The thin, vertical and horizontal bars on a window or a glazed door, that sub-divide window space into a number of smaller panes. The glass is held in place by glazier's SPRIGS or metal clips, and putty.

Also known as window bars.

GLAZING BEADS Strip of hardwood, with mitred corners, that are nailed or fixed with SCREWS and cups to secure panes of glass to GLAZING BARS. The glass is usually embedded in a strip of wash leather.

(◆ METAL WINDOWS)

GLIDES Fittings that can be attached to the bottom of furniture legs. Glides usually have a polished plastic or metal surface and reduce the friction between floor covering and furniture. They should not be used for furniture that needs to be moved frequently.

(♦ CASTORS)

GLOSS FINISH Paint that dries with a polished finish.

GLOSS PAINT ♦ PAINT

GOUGES Sharp, wood-cutting tools similar to CHISELS, but with curved steel blades that make them suitable for shaping hollows or rounded work.

The two kinds of gouge are:

Firmer This has two kinds of blade: the in-cannel and the out-cannel. The former has the bevelled cutting edge on the outside of the blade (the convex face), the latter on the inside face.

Useful sizes are 6 mm to 25 mm ($\frac{1}{4}$ in. to 1 in.) wide blades, 100 mm (4 ins.) long.

Paring A lighter, longer-bladed version of the firmer gouge. It is available in a range of thirteen different curve shapes, in blade widths from 6 mm to 32 mm ($\frac{1}{4}$ in. to $1\frac{1}{4}$ ins.), and is therefore suitable for cutting a greater variety of curved shapes.

GRANOLITHIC A flooring material that is usually laid IN SITU, consisting of CEMENT and fine, hard stone chippings. Carborundum and emery grains are sometimes added to give a grano' floor a non-slip finish.

GRANTS Financial grants are awarded by local councils to help owner-occupiers to improve or repair their properties (i.e. to bring dwellings up to a good standard of amenities) or to help towards the cost of converting large houses.

Grants are not normally available for dwellings built after 2 October 1961 (after 15 June 1964 in Scotland). The rateable value of a property also governs grant eligibility. In all cases details of the grants available in an area can be obtained by applying to the local council.

The types of grants available in England

and Wales are listed below; in Scotland and Northern Ireland the nature of the grants is slightly different.

Historic Buildings Money may be available to help owners pay for structural repairs to a LISTED BUILDING or one that is in a CONSERVATION AREA.

Improvement These are grants made at the discretion of local councils to help owners bring older properties up to standard (e.g. replace a DPC or strengthen FOUNDATIONS), or to help toward the cost of converting a large property into two or more self-contained dwellings.

Intermediate These are grants made by local councils to help toward the cost of installing any or all standard basic amenities, e.g. a bath or shower, a wash basin, a kitchen sink – with hot and cold water supplies to all, and a water closet.

An Intermediate Grant may also be available to provide alternative amenities for disabled occupants.

Repair These grants are available only to people of limited means, to help them finance essential repairs which they could not otherwise afford. Repair Grants do not embrace home improvement or conversion work, and are only available in *Housing Action Areas* and *General Improvement Areas*, at the discretion of local councils.

Special These are made at the discretion of the local council, for improvements to houses shared by one or more household – a single household sharing a property does not qualify.

A Special Grant is usually awarded for work on an old property that is not worth converting into separate flats, or where there is no immediate prospect of conversion work.

GRASSCLOTH ◗ WALL COVERINGS
GRAVITY CIRCULATION ◗ LOW PRESSURE SYSTEM

GRAVITY-FEED BOILER A solid fuel boiler that only needs to be topped up with fuel, by hand, on average once a day.

GRAVITY TOGGLE ♦ WALL FIXINGS

GRINDSTONE An abrasive disc of natural or synthetic stone (aluminium or silicon carbide) used on a hand- or power-operated machine for sharpening edge-cutting tools.

Discs are available in diameters from 125 mm to 250 mm (5 ins. to 10 ins.).

GROUND A piece of softwood used for fixing SKIRTING BOARDS and DOOR LININGS to walls. A skirting ground generally has a bevelled top to provide a keyed edge for plaster on a wall.

GROUT A liquid mix of CEMENT mortar used to fill holes and cavities in a brick or stone wall. Proprietary brands are available for filling joint lines between ceramic tiles.

(♦ WALL TILING)

GULLY A glazed earthenware fitting, with a TRAP, through which rainwater and any other surface water are conveyed to the DRAINS.

An open gully has a top with a metal grille, with a DOWNPIPE discharging into it from above. Pipes from a nearby sink or basin may also discharge into the same gully.

An inlet gully also has a grille, but the downpipe discharges into the gully below ground level – either at the side or the back of the fitting.

The advantage is that, while an open gully can become blocked with leaves and cause flooding, rainwater can still enter the drains through an inlet gully.

GUTTERS AND DOWNPIPES The principal fittings by which rainwater is conveyed from the roof of a house to gullies at ground level and then to the DRAINS. The gutters are fixed by brackets screwed to FASCIA boards; the downpipes by clips

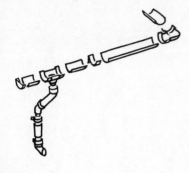

and backplates (holder-bats) plugged and screwed to the wall.

Downpipes may also incorporate a rainwater hopper – a funnel-shaped fitting that can be used to collect rainwater from another downpipe and/or waste water from a bath or basin outlet. Rainwater hoppers are common on old houses where there are complex roof shapes to be drained.

Gutters are made in three different cross sectional shapes: half round, rectangular and ogee.

Proprietary fittings are manufactured in plastic, ASBESTOS CEMENT, and metal – cast iron, pressed steel, aluminium, copper and zinc. Manufacturers of most systems supply detailed literature, illustrating the component parts and the jointing methods, which vary according to the material used.

(◆ BOX GUTTER; GULLY; VALLEY GUTTER)

H

HACKSAW ◗ SAWS

HALF-ROUND FILE ◗ FILES

HALVING JOINT A strong, neat and simple method of joining two pieces of wood of the same thickness, either crossways or lengthways. Each is cut to half its width or thickness, so that when the cut faces are glued and pinned (sometimes screwed) to each other the outer faces of both are flush.

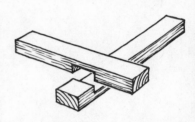

There are many variations of this multi-purpose joint.

HAMMERS The use of the right hammer can be the difference between a job being easy or difficult.

There are several different types, each suited to a particular range of jobs. For the average handyman the following are worth knowing about:

Claw A good all-round hammer for general carpentry work, with a claw that is invaluable for pulling out bent nails from wood. The curved claw is the most commonly used type, but a 'straight claw' (one that has the least curve) is suitable for lifting floorboards.

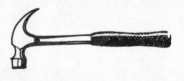

Available with steel or wooden handles and with steel heads up to 570 g (about 20 oz). See right.

Club A heavy-duty hammer suitable for breaking up masonry, or when using a cold chisel or a masonry bit to make wall fixings. See right.

Head weights up to 1.8 kg (4 lbs).

Cross pein So-called because the opposite side of the striking face on the head, is wedge-shaped. This is useful when starting

small nails in wood, before driving them home with the head. One type – of which there are several – is also known as a Warrington. See below left.

Head weights up to 455 g (16 oz).

Engineer's A hammer with a ball-shaped pein that is chiefly used for metalwork, e.g. when riveting. But engineer's hammers can also be bought with a straight pein (one in line with the shaft) and a cross-pein (at right angles to the shaft). See left.

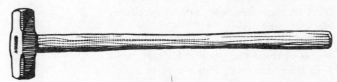

Sledge For really heavy work, such as driving home stakes or breaking up HARDCORE. Shaft lengths are up to 900 mm (about 3 ft) long, with head weights up to 9 kg (20 lbs). See above.

Veneer A specialist tool used to press down a wood veneer glued surface. It has a wooden head, with a broad edge grooved to receive a thin steel blade. See left.

HAND DRILL ♦ DRILLS

HANGER A vertical timber found on some roof trusses that is secured to, and hangs from, the RIDGE or PURLIN to reduce the weight – and thereby the size – of ceiling joists.

HARDBOARD A fibre building board, made in sheet form from compressed softwood pulp.

There are three grades: standard, medium and tempered. The first two are suitable for use internally, the third externally.

Standard hardboard has one smooth face (the finished side) and one textured, and is suitable for a multitude of jobs, from WALL CLADDING to built-in furniture.

Medium hardboard is a little softer and used more for non-decorative work, such as surfacing a STUD PARTITION.

Common sheet sizes are 1220 mm by 1830 mm to 3600 mm (4 ft by 6 ft to 12 ft) in 3.2 mm, 4.8 mm and 6.4 mm thicknesses.

Among the many other types of hardboard available there are:

Perforated studded with small holes for use as a decorative screen or peg-board.

Laminated surfaced with plastic, wood or metal veneers.

Embossed moulded or impressed with patterns to simulate other surfaces, such as cloth or wood grain.

HARDCORE Broken bricks, concrete blocks or stone that are consolidated as a foundation for oversite concrete in solid floors.

The average house has 150 mm (6 ins.) of hardcore beneath the concrete ground floor.

HARD WATER Water containing salts – calcium, magnesium and iron – that cause scale and fur to form on the inside of pipes and hot water cylinders, such as can be seen inside a kettle.

The effects of hard water can be cured with a WATER SOFTENER.

HARDWOODS The wood from deciduous trees, i.e. those which shed their leaves periodically, such as ash, beech, oak, walnut and others.

Hardwoods are generally used either for their decorative values, e.g. as veneers or for good quality joinery, or where the specific hard-wearing properties of hardwood are needed, such as floor finishes or bench tops.

(◗ SOFTWOOD)

HAWK A home-made tool useful for carrying small quantities of cement mortar or plaster to a wall while working on it.

A hawk consists of a piece of 6 mm (½ in.) thick plywood, about 300 mm

(12 ins.) square, screwed to a short length
of broom handle.

HEAD OF WATER The pressure of
water at any point in a plumbing system.
This is due to the difference in height
between that point – such as a tap or
shower – and the level of the water in the
storage cistern.

One foot of water equals 0.434 lb/sq in.
A tap that is 9 ft (2.74 m) below the level
of the water in the tank is described as
having a 9 ft head of water. For a shower
to be effective the minimum head –
without the assistance of a pump – is 3 ft
(about 1 m).

HEADER A brick laid with its length at
right angles to the wall, so that one of its
short faces is exposed.
(◊ BONDS; BRICKS; STRETCHER)

HEARTWOOD The timber which is cut
from the core of a tree trunk and is darker,
harder and denser than the encircling sap-
wood. Heartwood is valued for veneers
since it is less prone to disease and decay.

HEATERS Individual heaters are used
either as an alternative or a supplement to
a CENTRAL HEATING system, and are
available in a bewildering range of proprietary appliances embracing portable,
wall-hung and floor-standing types.

Basically, they all transmit heat by one
of two methods: convection or radiation.

Convector heaters work on the principle
that as air is warmed it rises, displaced by
cooler air which, in turn, is also warmed
and rises, and so on, creating a current of
heated air, known as convection.

Radiant heaters work on a principle
similar to that of an electric lamp, emitting
warm air directly from the heating source,
i.e. panel heaters or radiators.

Radiant-convector heaters combine both
methods. They have a range of elements –
electric or gas-fired – sending out radiant
heat, with cold air being drawn in at the

bottom of the casing, heated by the back of the elements, and escaping through grilles at the top of the casing to send out convected heat.

A fan convector draws cold air in at the back of the casing, which passes over electrically-heated elements, and is then blown out at the front as hot air.

HERRING-BONE BOND Flooring wood blocks or paving bricks arranged obliquely in alternate rows, to form a zig-zag pattern.

HERRING-BONE STRUTTING ◆ STRUTTING

HESSIAN ◆ WALL COVERINGS

HINGES There are over 200 different types of hinges manufactured, most of which are designed to satisfy specific design needs or practical requirements. An obvious but important consideration when buying hinges is to be sure they are able to support the full weight of a door or flap when it is fully opened out, or sagging will occur.

The size of a hinge is classified by its overall length and breadth when both leaves are opened out fully, i.e. at 180°.

Hinges are also described as left-hand, or right-hand. This is determined by looking at a hinge in the open position, with the countersunk side of the holes towards you. If the flap on the hinge (which is fixed to the door) is on your left, it is a lefthand hinge, and vice-versa.

The following hinges are a selection of some of the most useful types, manufactured in various materials. Generally speaking heavy hinges for heavy doors and gates are made of aluminium, brass, iron and steel; and lighter hinges for cabinet work are made of aluminium, brass, chromium plate or nickel, nylon and stainless steel.

Back-flap Hinges with large leaves used for fixings to the face of a door, when the door

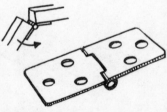

back-flap

is too thin for conventional butt hinges. Back-flap hinges are often used on drop-flap table tops and bureau flaps.

Butt The commonest hinge used for room and full-size cupboard doors. Butts are usually recessed into the door edge and frame so all surfaces are flush. See left.

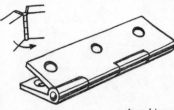

butt hinge

There are four different types of butt hinge: the fixed pin has both leaves permanently fixed at the knuckle; the loose-pin, which can be withdrawn so that the door can be taken off without unscrewing the hinges; the lift-off hinge, which is in two parts so that the door can be lifted off when necessary; and finally, the rising butt. This has a spiral fitting at the knuckle, designed so that when the door is opened it rises slightly, about 12 mm ($\frac{1}{2}$ in.), and clears the carpet. The door's own weight also helps it to close on its own.

concealed cylinder hinge

Like the lift-off hinge the rising butt is in two parts so that a door can easily be lifted off without unscrewing hinges.

Concealed There are several types of concealed or invisible hinges, designed so that when a door is closed the hinges cannot be seen – ideal for good class furniture.

Each hinge is recessed into both the door and the frame and can be bought to open at an angle of 90° or 180°.

Concealed hinges are suitable for cabinet work, such as folding or flap-down doors.

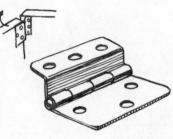

cranked hinge

Cranked Used on cabinet doors that fit on the outside of a frame, rather than within it, so that the doors can be opened at an angle of 180°. This type of hinge allows adjoining doors to be fully opened without fouling each other. Made with a fixed-pin or a loose-pin knuckle.

Flush-fitting A lightweight form of butt hinge, made in various patterns, but all designed so that one leaf fits snugly into the other when the door is closed. A flush-fitting hinge, therefore, does not

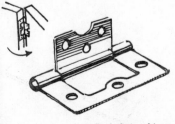

flush fitting hinge

73

need to be recessed into the door or frame. Unsuitable for full-size room or cupboard doors, but ideal for smaller cabinet doors.

Lay-on There are several types of lay-on hinge, all designed for cupboard doors that 'lay' on the surface of a frame. The type illustrated is the simplest – more sophisticated designs are spring-loaded and will hold a door open. See right.

Parliament A hinge that allows a full-size door to open at 180°. When the hinges are fixed, the knuckle and the reduced neck of the leaves projects from the wall, so that when the door is opened it swings out and away. See right.

Piano (or *Continuous*) As the name implies, this is a long hinge that can be bought in standard lengths up to 840 mm (roughly 33 ins.). See right.

It is used for fixing desk flaps, cabinet doors or chest lids.

Pivot Descriptive of a broad range of hinges that operate on the pivot principle. The type illustrated is a friction hinge, that is often used on windows. It enables a window (or door) to remain open in any position.

T-hinge (or *Cross-garnet*) A long mild steel strap hinge, fixed to the face of large LEDGED-AND-BRACED doors, or garden gates.

Wide-angle Hinges made to open doors at angles of between 100° and 180°, and to swing clear of any adjoining cabinet doors. There are many types of wide-angle hinge that are concealed and have a spring or catch mechanism.

HIPPED ROOF A roof with triangular ends that slope the same as the sides.

HIP TILES Specially manufactured tiles, which unlike most other roofing tiles do not overlap each other, but are BUTT-JOINTED to cover the hip joint.

The tiles may be half round or angular in section and are made of concrete or clay.

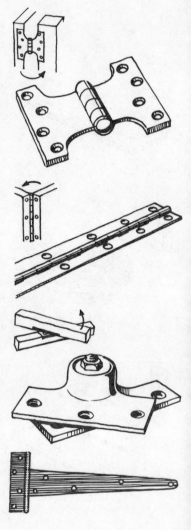

HISTORIC BUILDING GRANTS ▶
GRANTS
HOLDERBATS ▶ GUTTERS AND
DOWNPIPES
HOLDFAST A cramp-like tool used on a
woodworking bench to hold wood in place
while it is being worked. The tool fits into a
small metal collar, fixed in the bench top,
and can therefore be removed when not in
use.
HOLE SAW ▶ SAWS
HONEYCOMB BOND ▶ BONDS
HONING GAUGE A handy gadget that
is used when sharpening blades of chisels,
planes, etc. The gauge ensures the blade is
held at the correct angle.
 Can take blades from 3 mm to 57 mm
($\frac{1}{8}$ in. to $2\frac{1}{4}$ ins.) wide.
HOPPER HEAD ▶ GUTTERS AND
DOWNPIPES
HOT WATER CYLINDER A sealed
copper cylinder used to store hot water for
domestic purposes. There are two kinds of
cylinder: direct and indirect.
Direct Water is heated by the boiler (or an
IMMERSION HEATER) and drawn off at
the taps, with automatic replenishment
from the cold water storage cistern.
Indirect Also known as a calorifier, it has
another smaller cylinder inside it, which is
linked by a PRIMARY CIRCUIT (or closed
circuit) of pipework to the boiler. The hot
water in the smaller cylinder 'indirectly'
heats the water in the larger, providing the
supply needed for domestic purposes, including central heating.
 Although water from the inner cylinder
is never used, a small loss occurs due to
evaporation. There is also a need for water
to escape should overheating occur. Both
problems are overcome by a feed-and-
expansion tank. This is a small, open storage tank, usually in the roofspace, which is
supplied with water from the main storage
CISTERN.

A patent form of indirect cylinder that does away with the need for a separate feed-and-expansion tank, is the self-priming cylinder. Several types are manufactured and, although more costly than a conventional cylinder, they simplify plumbing pipework.

The purpose of an indirect cylinder is to limit hard water scaling that can fur up the inside of pipes and cylinders.

A cylinder with a storage capacity of 25 to 30 gallons will provide sufficient water for an average family's needs.

(◊ HARD WATER SCALING)

HOUSED JOINT A strong and rigid woodworking joint, where one board is recessed into another – the depth of the recess is no more than a third of the wood's thickness.

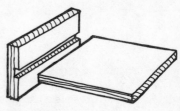

housed joint

A stopped housing has the recess cut to stop about 12 mm (½ in.) short of the front edge of the wood, so that the recess cannot be seen.

Both can be glued and pinned for extra strength and are suitable for shelving systems, but the stopped housing is the better looking joint of the two.

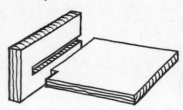

stopped housing

HOUSING ACTION AREAS Districts where existing physical and social conditions are so inadequate as to create unsatisfactory living conditions. In such areas, designated by local authorities, higher rates of GRANTS are available.

HUMIDIFIER An appliance that maintains and regulates the level of moisture in the air. The simplest kind has a trough of water beneath a raised absorbent surface and can be hung on a radiator to accelerate evaporation. More sophisticated humidifiers can be free-standing, incorporating a fan that distributes an atomized spray of moisture in a room.

IMMERSION HEATER An insulated electric element that can be fitted permanently into a HOT WATER CYLINDER. An immersion heater can be the sole method of heating water, or the secondary method used – in conjunction with CENTRAL HEATING – when the BOILER is closed down, i.e. during the summer months.

The heaters are manufactured with ratings from 1 kw to 3 kw, for cylinders having from 15 gallon to 50 gallon capacities.

An immersion heater must be permanently wired into a separate circuit, with its own 13 amp or 15 amp fuse, and a switch. It can be wired to use OFF-PEAK electricity.

A THERMOSTAT in the top of the heater can be set to one of three temperatures.

IMPACT ADHESIVE ▶ ADHESIVES

IMPACT DRIVER A tool used to free screws or nuts that have seized. The impact driver has replaceable heads to fit slotted or cross-head screws, and when struck with a hammer converts the force of the blow into a torque action to free the fitting.

Size is 140 mm (5½ ins.).

IMPROVEMENT GRANTS ▶ GRANTS

INDIRECT CYLINDER ▶ HOT WATER CYLINDER

INFRA-RED HEATER A radiant electric heater with a rod element inside a silica tube, mounted in front of a reflector.

It is a safe heater for a bathroom, if it is mounted permanently high up on a wall or ceiling, and is fitted with a pull-cord switch, or a switch control outside the bathroom.

Generally available in the range of 1 kw to 3 kw.

INGRAIN PAPER ▶ WALLPAPERS

IN SITU Generally used in connection with concrete that is placed, while still wet, in the place where it will remain when dry, e.g. floor slabs or garden paths. An in situ lintel is one cast in place.

INSPECTION CHAMBER (Manhole) A brick-built chamber, with a concrete base, provided at the junction of drainpipes in order to give access to the drains for cleaning or clearing blockages.

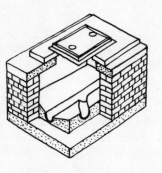

The chamber may be deep enough for a man to enter or as shallow as half a metre (about 18 ins.), according to the slope of the ground and the depth of the drain (sewer). The chamber is sealed with a close-fitting metal cover.

INSTANTANEOUS WATER HEATER An appliance that provides hot water as it is drawn off rather than storing it. There are two types of instantaneous water heater: one serving a single tap or a shower, or one known as a multi-point, serving several taps.

Either type can be electric or gas-fired. Electric heaters are available in ratings from 3 kW to 5 kW.

INSULATING FIBRE BOARDS ▶ INSULATION MATERIALS

INSULATING MATERIALS These fall into two groups: those that help to keep the heat in and the cold out of a house, and those that deaden sound transmitted through the structure, or insulate it internally from outside noises. Few materials are suitable for both thermal and acoustic insulation and the best results are often achieved by using them in combination.

Aluminium foil A thin sheet of aluminium bonded to one or more sides of Kraft paper is often used as a thermal insulator in roof or wall construction – the metallic surfaces act as reflectors.

Foil is most effectively used in sandwich construction, e.g. a timber-framed wall clad with clay tiles or horizontal boards.

Fibreboard Sheet materials made from wood or vegetable fibres, either compressed during manufacture to make strong and dense building boards (HARDBOARD), or left unpressed to form insulating boards.

Fibreboard may be used in roof or wall construction.

Lagging Narrow strips of felt or tubes of foam rubber that fit around water pipes to protect them from cold weather and save wasting heat.

Lagging is also used to insulate hot water cylinders.

Loose-fill Lightweight materials with a high insulation value, such as vermiculite, granulated cork, and mineral wool, that can be laid between floor or ceiling joists to keep in heat. Similar materials are also used in some forms of cavity infilling.

Mineral wool A warm, resilient and lightweight material made from slag or mineral fibres. Mineral wool varies in density according to the way it is used, either in semi-rigid slabs for insulating walls and roofs, as the stuffing in insulating mats or quilts, or when used as a loose-filling, e.g. when filling cavity walls.

Polystyrene Expanded polystyrene, i.e. foamed plastic, is a spongy, easily damaged material, with excellent thermal insulation properties.

It is available in a variety of forms: as a rigid sheet material for use with other slab materials, such as FIBRE BUILDING BOARD; as tiles for walls or ceilings; as beads of loose-fill insulation; and in rolls of 2 mm thick sheets, which can be used like wallpaper to help reduce the effects of condensation by raising the surface temperature.

Pugging Material put between the joists in a suspended wooden floor in order to deaden sound transmission.

Quilt Layers of Kraft paper stitched together with lightweight fillings of materials such as mineral wool, eel grass (the leaves of a dried sea plant), or grass silk, to make an insulation blanket or quilt. Quilting is used to insulate loft spaces, timber-framed walls, and as jackets for HOT WATER CYLINDERS.

Vermiculite This consists of expanded nodules of mica – a fire-resistant material with a low thermal conductivity. Ideal as a loose-fill insulation between joists in a roof space, or as an infilling material in a casing around a COLD WATER STORAGE TANK.

Vermiculite is also used to protect metals – sprayed on to the surface with an adhesive, or as a lightweight AGGREGATE in certain PLASTERS and flooring SCREEDS.

(♦ CAVITY WALLS)

INTERCEPTOR TRAP A water-filled trap between a domestic drainage system and the point where it enters the public sewer.

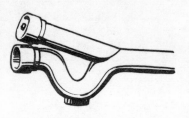

The trap – inside a small brick chamber for access purposes – prevents odours returning from the main sewer entering a house, and is often linked to a fresh air inlet.

Interceptor traps were once obligatory, but many local authorities will dispense with them if the design of a drainage system is adequately ventilated by other means.

INTERMEDIATE GRANTS ♦ GRANTS

INTERNAL CLADDING ♦ WALL CLADDING

INTERWOVEN FENCING Wood fencing consisting of panels of varying heights and 1.8 m (6 ft) wide, formed from thin slats of timber, interwoven together to form a solid screen. Panels are nailed to 75 mm (3 in.) square posts.

INVERT LEVEL The difference – often marked on an architect's or builder's site plan – between the bottom of an INSPECTION CHAMBER and the top of the lid.

IRONMONGERY A collective term, often used in a SPECIFICATION or a BILL OF QUANTITIES, which describes the metal fastenings and fittings – such as locks, catches, handles and hinges, etc – used on doors and windows.

ITALIAN (ROMAN) TILING A combination of two types of clay roofing tiles. The undertiles – known in the trade as 'unders' – are flat, tray-like tiles with their long edges turned up at right angles, linked and covered by 'overs' – half-round and tapered tiles.

(◆ SPANISH TILING)

J

JACK PLANE ♦ PLANES
JAMB The vertical sides of an opening in a wall or fireplace.
JENNINGS-PATTERN AUGER ♦ BITS
JIG SAW ♦ SAWS
JOINTING The method of finishing the joints between brick COURSES, as the work proceeds, by using the same mortar as that used to lay bricks.
   Compare with POINTING.
JOISTS Horizontal timbers, deeper than they are wide, that span structural walls to support floors and ceilings, and to frame staircase openings.
JOIST HANGERS Pressed steel shoes, which can be built into a flush-faced brick or blockwork wall, to provide supports for the ends of joists. See right.

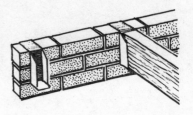

JUMPER Part of the internal mechanism of a water TAP, to which a washer is attached to make it watertight.
JUNCTION BOX A circular box, containing four terminals, which provides the means of linking electric CABLE above a ceiling or between floor JOISTS.
JUNIOR HACKSAW ♦ SAWS

KEENE'S CEMENT A slow-drying plaster that can be used for the finishing coat on a cement-RENDERED base to achieve a hard, smooth finish. Also known as Parian plaster, it is useful for finishing corners.

KEEPER PLATE A metal plate – with one or more rectangular holes in it – that is screwed to a DOOR LINING or DOOR FRAME, so that the LATCH or LOCK engages in it when the door is closed.

It is also known as the striker or striking plate. See left.

KERFING A series of parallel, half-depth saw cuts, made in the thickness of a piece of wood to enable it to be curved.

KEYED BRICK ◗ BRICKS

KEYED JOINT ◗ POINTING

KEYHOLE PLATE ◗ ESCUTCHEON

KEYHOLE SAW ◗ SAWS

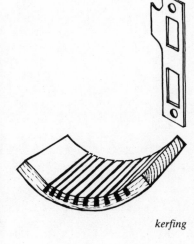

kerfing

KEYSTONE The central stone at the crown (or top) of an arch, which is the last one to be placed.

KILOWATT (kW) A unit of electric power – 1000 WATTS – expressed as kW.

KING CLOSER ◗ CLOSER

KITE WINDER The kite-shaped tread on a staircase that turns at a right angle. There are usually three treads at this point, springing from a NEWEL or upright post. The central tread is the kite winder.

KNAPPED FLINT Flints that have been knapped, i.e. snapped in half with a knapping hammer. Knapped flints are usually built into a wall, with the dark snapped faced exposed – the wall is framed by courses of brickwork or contrasting stone.

KNOCKED DOWN A term used to describe manufactured building components that can be supplied with all parts complete, including fittings, ready for self-assembly.

Often known as KD units.

KNOTTING Sealing knots in new woodwork with a solution of shellac and methylated spirits, in order to prevent natural resins bleeding out and affecting subsequent polish or decoration.

KNOTS The parts of branches embedded in timber. Dead or loose knots – those which are not joined to the surround timber – can affect the strength of the wood. Pin knots – less than 3 mm ($\frac{1}{8}$ in.) in diameter – and those which are tight, sound and free of decay are harmless.

KRAFT PAPER Thin, tough, brown paper used with insulation materials to make insulation blankets.

(◆ INSULATING MATERIALS)

kW ◆ KILOWATT

LACED VALLEY A junction between two sloping roofs that is joined and water-proofed with tiles or slates 'knitted' together. A laced valley is formed with special width tiles or slates laid over a wide board. Compare with SWEPT VALLEY.
(◊ VALLEY GUTTER)

LAGGING ◊ INSULATION MATERIALS

LAMBSWOOL BONNET ◊ POWER TOOL ATTACHMENTS

LAMBSWOOL ROLLER ◊ PAINT ROLLERS

LAMINATED PLASTIC A rigid (though brittle), stain-proof and durable material, used primarily for surfacing worktops, shelves and furniture.

It is made from sheets of plain or patterned paper or fabric impregnated with a synthetic resin and bonded together under pressure with a film of strong, transparent plastic.

It is manufactured in various thicknesses and grades – the common thickness being 1.5 mm ($\frac{1}{16}$ in.) – and can be bought cut to size or in large sheets, 3050 mm by 1220 mm (about 10 ft by 4 ft).

LAMINBOARD A manufactured board, similar to BLOCKBOARD but stronger and more expensive, generally used on high quality work that is to be veneered.

Laminboard has a core of softwood strips, between 3 mm and 6 mm (roughly $\frac{1}{8}$ in. to $\frac{1}{4}$ in.) wide; all glued and bonded together under pressure and sandwiched between one or two veneers of hardwood.

Laminboard is manufactured in similar

sheet sizes to blockboard but no more than 9 mm ($\frac{3}{8}$ in.) thick.

LAPPED JOINT ◊ END-TO-END JOINTS

LATCH ◊ LOCKS AND LATCHES

LATEX ADHESIVE ◊ ADHESIVES

LATH AND PLASTER Sawn or split strips of timber – often Baltic fir – about 25 mm by 6 mm (1 in. by $\frac{1}{4}$ in.) – nailed to the timber uprights on a STUD PARTITION wall. The strips are fixed with 10 mm ($\frac{3}{8}$ in.) spaces between them, to provide a key for PLASTER. Also used for ceilings.

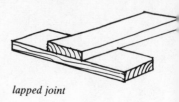

lapped joint

Lath and plaster has been largely superseded by sheets of PLASTERBOARD.

LATHE A machine used to 'turn' wood into cylindrically shaped objects, such as furniture legs.

LAY-ON HINGE ◊ HINGES

LEADED LIGHT A window with QUARRELS – small diamond or square-shaped panes of glass – held together by cames (strips of lead).

LEAN-TO A structure, usually built on to the side of a house (such as a garage or covered passage), with a single-sloped roof.

LEDGED-AND-BRACED DOOR A sturdy and traditional door made from lengths of tongued-and-grooved boards, fitted together and strengthened with horizontal ledges and diagonal braces.

LENGTHENING JOINTS ◊ END-TO-END JOINTS, EDGE-TO-EDGE JOINTS

LEVEL ◊ SPIRIT LEVEL

LEVELLING PEG Pointed wooden stake with a flat top, used on sites for establishing levels, such as trench levels or finished floor levels.

LEVELLING SCREED A fine grade mixture of SAND and CEMENT, which is mixed with water to the consistency of single cream and trowelled over the surface of a concrete floor to provide a smooth finish for tiling or carpeting. Levelling screeds, despite the name, will not make a sloping floor level – they are merely self-smoothing.

Also known as smoothing compounds, levelling-screed mixtures can be bought in 20 kg (about 56 lb) bags from builders' merchants.

LIME Chalk or calcium carbonate that has been burnt in a kiln to produce quick-lime. When this is slaked with water it produces hydrated lime. It is this, when used as an additive to CEMENT MORTARS, that causes them to harden slowly and attain a slight elasticity, sufficient to reduce the excessive shrinkage that might otherwise appear.

LINCRUSTA ◗ WALL COVERINGS

LINING ◗ DOOR LINING

LINING PAPER ◗ WALLPAPERS

LINOLEUM A hard-wearing, resilient, and easy to clean material that is among the most economical of floor coverings.

Linoleum is manufactured from natural oils, cork, wood powders, and pigments, mixed and bonded under pressure to a backing material of either jute canvas or bituminized felt/paper.

Linoleum is available in sheet and tile form in a fair range of colours. Thicknesses vary from between 2 mm and 4.5 mm (roughly $\frac{1}{16}$ in. and $\frac{3}{16}$ in.) with the sheet material in standard 1.8 m (roughly 2 yd) widths; and the tiles in 300 mm (12 in.) squares.

LINSEED OIL The product of crushed seeds of flax. Used for painting and varnishing.

LINTEL A short beam across an opening, such as a door or window, carrying the weight of part of the wall directly above it. In some cases a lintel may also support part of the floor above.

Lintels may be made of PRECAST CONCRETE, REINFORCED CONCRETE, or be cast IN SITU.

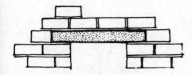

Another type available is the pressed steel lintel. This is made of lightweight galvanized metal and is shaped in such a way that it also acts as a DAMP-PROOF COURSE.

LIPPING In order to provide a more decorative edge to manufactured boards, such as blockboard, strips of hardwood or softwood are fixed to the exposed edges.

Lipping also has a practical value, providing a more substantial material for securing hinges or similar fixings.

LISTED BUILDING Any building that is considered to be of architectural or historic interest is classified as a Listed Building. As such, special consent must be applied for before any alteration may be made that might affect the building's character or appearance.

LIVE EDGE The edge of an area of paint that is wet enough to blend with additional paint, without forming an unsightly line or ridge.

LOAD BEARING Any part of a structure that supports more than its own weight.

LOCATION PLAN A drawing that shows the position of a building on its site, the boundaries of that site, and the principal dimensions and features on the site.

LOCK NUT A second nut, screwed on to a bolt in order to ensure that the first nut does not work loose. A lock nut may have a split pin to secure it.

LOCK RAIL The middle rail of a panelled door that carries the door lock. In a FLUSH DOOR, the lock is fixed to a lock block – a piece of softwood fitted within the thickness of the framework.

LOCKS AND LATCHES There are four basic types in common use:
Latch A spring-loaded bolt which is drawn back by turning a lever handle or knob. A latch keeps a door closed but does not provide security.

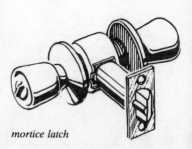

mortice latch

Dead lock A single bolt that is turned solely by the use of a key.

Two-bolt lock A combination of latch and dead lock – the most common form of internal door lock.

Night latch (or *Cylinder night latch*) This has a spring-loaded bolt, but is operated from inside by a lever handle or knob and from the outside by a key (also known as a Yale lock).

night latch

The latch has a sliding catch that can secure the latch when closed (or open), and it cannot then be operated by the key.

Rim locks and latches are those which are fixed to the surface of a door; mortise locks and latches are set within the thickness of a door. Mortise fittings provide greater security but are more expensive, and can only be fitted to doors of reasonable thickness, e.g. a 13 mm ($\frac{1}{2}$ in.) thick lock needs a 35 mm ($1\frac{3}{8}$ ins.) thick door.

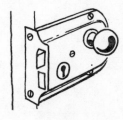

rim lock and latch

(◆ NORFOLK LATCH)

LOCKSHIELD VALVE There are two valves on a radiator, one used by the householder to switch the radiator on and off, the other – the lockshield valve – preset by the engineer when the central heating system is installed. The lockshield valve controls the amount of water passing through the radiator and should only ever need be set once. Hence, it is fitted with a protective cap to prevent any further adjustment being made.

(◆ VALVES)

LOFT LADDER A lightweight metal or timber ladder, fixed to a trap door in an upper-floor ceiling to provide access to the loft space. The ladder retracts into the loft and cannot be seen when the door is closed.

Loft ladders are available in a variety of designs but are basically either telescopic – operated manually – or single ladders, counterbalanced by an arrangement of weights and springs.

LOOSE-FILL ◊ INSULATION
MATERIALS
LONG-NOSE PLIERS ◊ PLIERS
LOST-HEAD NAIL ◊ NAILS
LOUVRE DOOR A door fitted with louvres – inclined horizontal slats of wood that let air in but also maintain visual privacy.

Mock-louvres are sometimes used, where the decorative effect of real louvres is wanted, to keep out dust and sound.
LOW-PRESSURE SYSTEM The natural means by which heated water rises in a plumbing system without the benefit of a CIRCULATION PUMP. As water is heated its density is reduced and it rises above the cold water.

It is sometimes referred to as a gravity circulation system.

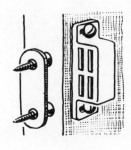

M

MADE-UP GROUND Soil that has been used to build up new levels or excavated parts of a site that have been filled in with earth.

MAGNETIC CATCH A furniture door catch, consisting of two parts: one contains a magnet and is fixed to the door frame or carcassing; the other is a metal plate screwed to the door.

Magnetic catches vary in design but there are two main types: rectangular and cylindrical.

MAINS SUPPLY The gas or water pipe, or electricity cable that brings the supply into a house from the appropriate authority's supply pipe or cable in the road.

(◗ RISING MAIN)

MAINS' TESTER SCREWDRIVER
◗ SCREWDRIVERS

MAKE GOOD To repair damage or improve bad workmanship.

MALLET A wooden hammer used for general carpentry work, where a conventional metal hammer might damage the work or any tool that is being struck, such as a CHISEL.

Head sizes from 65 mm to 175 mm ($2\frac{1}{2}$ ins. to 7 ins. approximately).

MANHOLE ◗ INSPECTION CHAMBER

MANIPULATIVE JOINT ◗ COMPRESSION JOINT

MAN-MADE BOARDS ◗ BLOCKBOARD; CHIPBOARD; FIBRE BUILDING BOARD; HARDBOARD; LAMINBOARD; PLYWOOD

MARKING GAUGE ◗ GAUGES

91

MARQUETRY Different wood veneers used to form pictures or decorative patterns on the surface of wood.

MASONRY BIT ♦ BITS

MASONRY BOLT ♦ ANCHOR BOLT

MASONRY JOINT ♦ POINTING

MASONRY NAIL ♦ NAILS

MASONRY PAINT ♦ PAINTS

MASTIC A non-hardening material that is used to fill the joints between certain building elements, such as a door or window frame and the surrounding wall, to make a dust-, draught- and moistureproof seal. The mastic – which dries with a semi-hard protective skin – remains flexible enough to accommodate movement in the structure without cracking.

Some types of mastic can be painted.

Mastic is also made for sealing joints in pipework, rainwater fittings and EXPANSION JOINTS.

MASTIC GUN A metal tool, with a nozzle, used to apply MASTIC to joints around door and window frames. A replaceable cartridge of mastic is fitted in the gun and the contents forced out, through the nozzle, under pressure.

MATCH BOARDING ♦ TONGUED-AND-GROOVED BOARDING

MATT FINISH The dull finish that certain paints or varnishes may have when they dry.

MAT WELL A recess in the floor, usually by a front entrance door, to accommodate a rubber or coconut mat. The recess may be edged with hardwood strip, brass, or galvanized iron.

MECHANICAL CATCH A door catch consisting of two parts – one fixed to the frame and one to the door – connecting, when closed, by a spring-loaded peg or roller.

There are many variations of this principle.

MEETING RAILS The uprights that come together when a pair of doors is closed.

MELAMINE A clear synthetic resin used in the manufacturing process to give plastic laminates a tough, protective finish that can be cleaned easily.
(♦ LAMINATED PLASTIC)

METAL FLOAT ♦ FLOATS

METAL WINDOWS In houses metal windows are generally either mild steel or aluminium. Both kinds are available in a wide range of standard sizes and combination of types, and need little maintenance.

Steel windows are zinc-coated during manufacture to prevent them from corrosion, but still need the protection of a coat of paint.

Aluminium windows do not need painting except in areas where there is excessive pollution in the atmosphere; but they are more expensive than steel.

Both types are easy to fix – either directly to brickwork or to wooden or steel sub-frames.

MICROBORE ♦ CENTRAL HEATING

MINERAL WOOL ♦ INSULATING MATERIALS

MINIATURE CIRCUIT BREAKER (MCB) ♦ FUSES

MINIBORE ♦ CENTRAL HEATING

MINI-HACKSAW ♦ SAWS

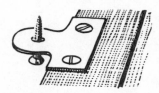

MIRROR PLATES Proprietary fittings, made of brass or chromium-plated metal, having three fixing holes – one sometimes keyhole-shaped.

The plates are screwed to the back of a mirror or picture frame, or a lightweight cupboard, so that the keyhole portion projects and can be slotted over a screw or similar fixture in the wall.

MIRROR TILES Squares of plain or decorative mirrors 300 mm (12 ins.) by 2.5 mm ($\frac{3}{32}$ in.) thick. The tiles are available with square or bevelled edges, and have

93

self-adhesive material on the back enabling them to be fixed to wall surfaces.

MITRE BOX A U-shaped assembly of beech wood or cast iron, used to guide a saw when cutting 45° angles for a MITRED JOINT, or right-angled joints in timber and metal.

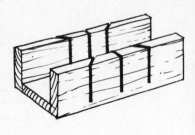

   Available in 225 mm and 300 mm (roughly 9 in. and 12 in.) lengths.

MITRE CRAMP ◗ CRAMPS

MITRED JOINT Two pieces of wood of the same size and section, cut at 45° and joined together to form a right angle.

MITRE SHOOTING BOARD ◗ SHOOTING BOARD

MIXER TAP ◗ TAPS

MIXER VALVE A control valve that mixes hot and cold water to provide a supply at a tap or shower head at the required temperature. Mixer valves vary in their cost and performance.

MOHAIR ROLLER ◗ PAINT ROLLERS

MOISTURE BARRIER A DAMP-PROOF COURSE or a CAPILLARY GROOVE which resists the passage of dampness.

MOISTURE CONTENT All wood contains moisture – the amount is expressed as a percentage of the wood's dry weight. Timber with a 10 per cent moisture content is suitable for most general purposes; used in a centrally-heated house it will eventually drop to about 8 per cent. It is therefore worth storing timber in a room where it is to be used for about a month beforehand to avoid subsequent shrinkage.

   Timber with a moisture content of 20 per cent or more is vulnerable (when used in unventilated conditions) to the effects of DRY ROT.

MOISTURE METER An instrument, used by damp-proofing specialists, that measures the amount of moisture present in a wall.

MOLE WRENCH ◗ WRENCHES

MONKEY GRIP ♦ WRENCHES

MORTAR Cement, lime and sand mixed together in varying proportions, according to the type and strength of the materials to be joined.

Cement mortar, i.e. sand and cement mixed in proportions of 3:1 (three parts sand to one of cement) is strong and sets rapidly, but will crack with shrinkage and settlement movements. It is used chiefly therefore for sills and copings and walls below DPC level.

The addition of lime reduces drying shrinkage, makes a more easily worked mortar and gives it a greater degree of elasticity to absorb minor shrinkage movements.

Mixtures of 1:1:6 (cement:lime:sand) and 1:2:9 (cement:lime:sand) are suitable for both internal and external brick walls.

MORTISE-AND-TENON JOINT
The strongest of all T-joints, it is usually used on door and window frames, and all good quality furniture.

MORTISE CHISEL ♦ CHISELS
MORTISE GAUGE ♦ GAUGES
MORTISE LOCKS AND LATCHES
♦ LOCKS AND LATCHES

MOSAICS Small square, rectangular or hexagonal-shaped tiles, made of clay, ceramic, marble or glass, and used for surfacing walls and floors – often in lavatories, bathrooms and utility rooms.

Mosaics are manufactured in a wide range of colours and with glazed or matt finishes, smooth or rustic faces, and non-slip textures suitable for floors.

Mosaic tiles – usually about 6 mm (¼ in.) thick – are sold on paper-backed panels 305 mm and 610 mm by 305 mm (1 ft and 2 ft by 1 ft) for ease of handling. The panels are fixed, tile side to the wall or floor, with special adhesive. When this is dry the paper is soaked off and the joints

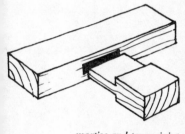

mortise-and-tenon joint

95

between the mosaics filled with GROUT – a waterproof compound.
(♦ TERRAZZO)

MOULDING PLANE ♦ PLANES

MOULDINGS Square or rectangular strips of timber – usually hardwood – which have been shaped on a machine for decorative purposes. Mouldings may be formed with concave and convex curves, recesses, grooves and rebates – either singly or in combinations of different types.

With built-in furniture and fittings, mouldings often have a functional purpose – to conceal the gaps between adjacent timbers that invariably shrink and would otherwise spoil the appearance of the job.

MOUSE A small strip of lead, tied to the end of a length of string, that is used when renewing a cord on a double-hung SASH WINDOW. The weighted string is passed over one of the two wheels, at the top of the sides of the window frame, and the other end of the string is tied to the new sash cord. It can then be pulled through the hollow space (or pocket) in the frame and secured to one of the counterbalance weights.

MULLIONS The vertical dividers in window openings and frames. Mullions, also known as munnions, may be made of stone, timber or metal.

MULTI-POINT HEATER ♦ INSTAN-TANEOUS WATER HEATER

MUNTIN The vertical dividers in a panelled door, mortised into the horizontal rails.

NAIL PUNCH A steel tool, with a square-ground tip, used with a hammer to punch nail heads below the surface of wood.

Point diameters vary from 0.5 mm to 4.5 mm, with a shaft 100 mm (4 ins.) long.

NAILS These vary greatly in shape, size, material and finish according to the job they are intended for. A selection of those in common use is as follows:

Annular nail A fastener with a series of ringed serrations along the shank. When the nail is hammered home, the sharp serrations bite into the wood, providing an irreversible grip.

Cheaper than screws, annular nails cannot however be withdrawn.

They are suitable for flooring, roofing and fencing work and available from 25 mm to 100 mm (1 in. to 4 ins.) long.

Clout A short, galvanized nail with a large, flat, round head used for fixing slates, roofing felt and the cords on SASH WINDOWS.

Clouts range from 9.5 mm to 63 mm ($\frac{3}{8}$ in. to $2\frac{1}{2}$ ins.) long.

Flooring brad (Cut floor nail) A nail of even thickness but tapered in its length and with a projecting head. It has a blunt tip and is suitable for fixing floorboards, since it will not split the wood, and is also easy to withdraw.

Sizes from 38 mm to 75 mm ($1\frac{1}{2}$ ins. to 3 ins.) long.

Lost head nail A nail with a comparatively small head that can be punched home below the surface of the wood and filled.

Used for general purpose joinery and flooring, in sizes ranging from 12 mm to 150 mm ($\frac{1}{2}$ in. to 6 ins.) long.

Hardboard pin Used for fixing hardboard, it has a diamond-shaped head that can be driven into the board. Sizes from 20 mm to 38 mm ($\frac{3}{4}$ in. to $1\frac{1}{2}$ ins.) long.

Masonry nail An extra hard nail that can be hammered into brick and masonry. Sizes range from 20 mm to 100 mm ($\frac{3}{4}$ in. to 4 ins.) long.

Oval wire nail Suitable for general purpose carpentry. It will not split the wood, providing the nail is driven home so that the longest axis of the nail head is in line with the grain.

Available in sizes from 20 mm to 150 mm ($\frac{3}{4}$ in. to 6 ins.) long.

Panel pin Small, thin, round nail, with a small head, used where inconspicuous fixings are needed for quality cabinet and joinery work, and for fixing MOULDINGS.

Sizes vary from 12 mm to 50 mm ($\frac{1}{2}$ in. to 2 ins.).

Sprig Small, headless nail – wedge-shaped – used to hold glass in place, in a frame, before puttying.

Sizes from 12 mm to 20 mm ($\frac{1}{2}$ in. to $\frac{3}{4}$ in.).

Staples U-shaped nails with two points, used to secure cable or wire to timber surfaces. Available in galvanized and plasticized finishes in a range of sizes.

Wire nail Flat, round-head nail, useful for general purpose work where the finished appearance is of secondary importance, since the head cannot be concealed.

Sizes from 20 mm to 150 mm ($\frac{3}{4}$ in. to 6 ins.).

NATURAL BED Stone that is laid so that its laminates or lines of stratification are horizontal. Stones laid this way contribute their greatest compressive strength.

NATURAL STONE Stone that has been quarried from the earth, as opposed to artificial or reconstructed stone, which is often used as a cheaper alternative for facing external walls.

NEWEL CAP A plain, carved or decorated piece of wood fixed to the top of a NEWEL POST.

NEWEL POST A stout post – often 100 mm (4 ins.) square – which is an integral part of the junction between flights of stairs and a floor or landing.

There may also be a newel post at the bottom of a staircase. In addition to playing a vital part in the structural stability of a staircase, newel posts also provide fixings for handrails.

NIBS Projections on the underside of a roofing tile, which hook over a TILING BATTEN.

NIGHT LATCH ♦ LOCKS AND LATCHES

NIGHT STORAGE HEATING ♦ CENTRAL HEATING

NOGGINGS Pieces of wood that are fixed, horizontally, between the uprights in a timber-frame (or STUD) partition, to give it extra rigidity and strength.

Noggings are usually the same section timber as the uprights, and are fixed to them with nails.

NOMINAL CAPACITY The total amount that, for example, a CISTERN is able to contain before it overflows at its brim.

A cistern with, say, a nominal capacity of 50 gallons has an *actual* capacity that is slightly less, due to the differences in level between the top of the cistern and OVERFLOW pipe.

NOMINAL SIZE The size of timber before it is machined smooth. The machining process reduces the size of wood slightly, thus: a piece of 25 mm (1 in.) square softwood is the nominal size. But the finished (or prepared) size is about 22 mm ($\frac{7}{8}$ in.) square.

If, when buying wood, the finished size is critical, timber must be prepared from the next size up and will therefore be, proportionally, more expensive.

NON-CONCUSSIVE TAP ♦ TAPS

NON-DRIP PAINT ♦ PAINTS

NON-LOAD-BEARING A wall that does no structural work other than support its own weight.

NON-MANIPULATIVE JOINT ♦ COMPRESSION JOINT

NON-RETURN VALVE A valve in a water pipe that permits water to flow in one direction only. The valve may be spring-assisted or operated by gravity.

NORFOLK LATCH A door fastener, consisting of a bar and catch on one side of the door, and a handle and thumb lift on the other. The thumb lift passes through a hole in the door and, when depressed by thumb pressure, raises the bar on the other side, clear of the catch.

A Norfolk latch was once used a great deal on LEDGED-AND-BRACED DOORS in East Anglian farmhouses and cottages.

It is also known as a thumb latch and Suffolk latch.

NOSING The leading edge of a TREAD (step) on a staircase – usually rounded.

NOSING LINE An imaginary straight line that connects all the NOSINGS on a staircase. It is from the nosing line that the minimum permissible headroom, specified by BUILDING REGULATIONS, is measured.

NOTCHED SPREADER This may be a purpose-made FLOAT, or a piece of metal or plastic with one or more serrated edges, used for spreading adhesive.

O

OFF-CUT The unwanted portions that are left after joints or shapes have been cut in a piece of wood. A selection of off-cuts kept in a bag can be useful for a variety of odd jobs when doing joinery or carpentry work.

OFF-PEAK TARIFF Electricity that is available at cheap rates during off-peak times, usually the 8 hour period between 11.00 p.m. and 7.00 a.m. This tariff is particularly suitable for night storage heating.

A white meter has a time switch that automatically changes from day-time tariff to off-peak tariff – so that whatever appliance is used during the night is charged for at the cheaper rate.

A quarterly charge is imposed for off-peak tariffs to cover the rental of the time switch and meter.

OFFSET ◆ WEATHERING

OGEE A moulding that has two curves forming a slender S-shape – one concave, the other convex.

OHM The unit of electrical resistance.

OIL-BASED PAINT ◆ PAINTS

OIL-FILLED RADIATOR A panel radiator that is filled with static oil, heated by an internal electric element. Oil-filled radiators often have integral thermostats and can be bought as wall-mounted or portable free-standing heaters that plug into ordinary SOCKET OUTLETS. (◆ HEATERS)

OIL-FIRED BOILER ◆ CENTRAL HEATING

OIL PAINT ◆ PAINTS

OILSTONE A quartz or carborundum stone that is used for sharpening cutting tools, such as chisels and planes. An oilstone may be coarse, medium or fine, or a combination of two grades – usually medium on one side and fine on the other.

The surface of an oilstone must be lubricated with light oil.
(◆ SLIPSTONES)

ONE-PIPE SYSTEM A drainage system used in some houses, where waste water and soil (sewage) water are fed into a single pipe.

A smaller pipe is sometimes necessary to provide ventilation to the system and prevent siphonage emptying the water in trapped fittings, such as a basin or lavatory.
(◆ ANTI-SIPHONAGE PIPE; TRAPS)

OPEN EAVES The overhanging edge of a roof that does not have a soffit board, thus exposing the underside of the rafters. The wall is built up between the rafters to weatherproof the roof-space and keep out nesting birds.

OPEN FIRE A fireplace that is independent of a BACK-BOILER or CENTRAL HEATING system, burning fuel in an open grate.

OPENING LIGHTS The parts of a window that can be opened.

OPEN PLAN A house that has been designed or converted so that it has few walls, if any, separating rooms. Open planning generally applies to ground floors only, with kitchen, living and dining rooms without dividing walls, to create the effect of spaciousness.

OPEN RISER A staircase that has TREADS but no RISERS. The treads are usually slightly thicker than conventional ones (to compensate for the lack of risers and the rigidity they contribute) and the distance between them is governed by BUILDING REGULATIONS.

Although hazardous for small children,

an open riser staircase eliminates dark areas underneath it.

OPEN WELL A staircase that has an open space between the flights as they rise from floor to floor, or floor to landing.

ORIEL WINDOW A window that projects from a wall – usually on an upper storey – and is supported by brackets or CORBELLING brickwork.

ORBITAL SANDER ◆ SANDING MACHINES

O-RING JOINT A method used to joint plastic pipes so that the joints are waterproof but remain slightly flexible. A rubber ring fits partly into a half-round groove around the socket of a pipe. The spigot on the end of the joining pipe is then lubricated with petroleum jelly and pushed almost fully into the socket.

OVAL WIRE NAIL ◆ NAILS

OVERFLOW A pipe that leads from a CISTERN to an outer wall, so that if a BALL VALVE sticks or fails, and a cistern starts to overflow, internal flooding will not occur. An overflow also acts as a warning sign.

OVERHANGING EAVES The foot of a sloping roof that projects beyond the face of the wall beneath it. Seldom used on a flat roof.

OVERSAILING ◆ CORBELLING

OVERSITE CONCRETE The concrete slab covering the HARDCORE on the ground floor of a building.

Oversite concrete is usually 100 mm to 150 mm (4 ins. or 6 ins.) thick, and provides the sub-surface for the DAMP-PROOF MEMBRANE and floor finish construction.

P

PADSAW ▸ SAWS

PADSTONE A natural stone or reinforced concrete block, built into a wall to
provide a bearing surface for a structural
beam, such as a PURLIN.

PALINGS The vertical stakes or boards
used in making a fence.

PAINT Paint consists of three consti-
tuents: pigment, binder, and thinner.

Pigment This is the finely ground
material – obtained from metals, minerals
and synthetic substances – that gives paint
its colour and opacity. Some pigments have
additional special qualities, such as rust
inhibitors.

Binder Also known as the medium or
vehicle, it is the resinous or gummy substance that binds the particles of paint
pigment together.

Thinner The fluid used to reduce the vis-
cosity of paints (and varnishes) to make
them more workable and easier to apply.
The usual thinner for an oil-based paint is
white spirit.

Paintwork usually consists of three different types of coats: primer, undercoat and
finishing coat.

Primer The first coat of paint put on new
woodwork or metalwork that is to be
finished with an oil-based paint. The primer seals the material and provides a surface
for subsequent coats to adhere to. Primers
vary according to the type of material
being painted, e.g. an acrylic primer is
suitable for softwood; alkali-resistant primer for plaster, concrete, brick, asbestos; a
metal primer, such as zinc chromate, for

most metals; and an aluminium wood primer for hardwood or resinous wood that is particularly oily. Other primers are manufactured for specific purposes.

Undercoat The coat or coats of paint used after the primer and before the finishing coats, or over previously painted work as a base for a new finishing coat.

Undercoat, which is usually a similar colour to the finishing coat but with a matt surface, helps to obliterate the colour of the primer or previous finish. It also provides a firm base for the finishing coat and an extra protective skin.

Although one undercoat is common practice, two or even three coats are often used on woodwork for a good class job.

Finish The final coat of paint that gives a workpiece its decorative appearance.

There are many varied types of paint manufactured for a wide variety of different purposes. A selection of the more common types is as follows:

Anti-condensation A heavy-bodied paint, containing absorbent pigments, which helps to reduce (but not cure) the effects of condensation on walls and ceilings. The paint absorbs some of the moisture until it can dry out. This type of paint is only effective, however, where condensation is intermittent and mild.

Bituminous A useful paint to use on surfaces that are vulnerable to corrosion, such as unprotected ferrous metals.

The paint also has water-repellent properties and is therefore suitable as a coating – where appearance is of secondary importance – for brickwork, concrete and timber. Bituminous paint is only available in dark colours due to the asphalt content, and unless the surface is coated with a metallic SEALER, it cannot be painted without 'BLEEDING' through.

Cement A white, cement-based paint suitable for giving a durable finish to brickwork, cement, or concrete and other similar porous surfaces. It is sold in powder form and must be mixed with water for application.

Emulsion A water-based paint that can be bought ready to use, or, in some cases, needs to be thinned with water before application. Many types of emulsion have synthetic additives – acrylic or vinyl, or a combination of both – which help give the paint a hardwearing and more durable surface, which is also stain-resistant and washable.

Emulsion paint is suitable for all indoor surfaces. Some types can be used externally. Emulsion – which is available in a matt, mid-sheen, silk or glossy finish – can sometimes be used as an undercoat for oil-based paints.

Fungicidal Paint that includes substances that do not provide food for fungi to feed on, and are therefore ideal in situations where mould or fungi growths might otherwise flourish.

Insecticidal Paint that includes substances that are poisonous to insects, such as bugs and cockroaches.

Lead-based These are largely superseded as traditional wood primers, because of their toxic nature.

Masonry Oil-based and emulsion paints that include additives to increase the body and durability of paint, suitable for external wall decorations. There are many different proprietary brands made, some containing minute particles of nylon, synthetic rubber-based resins, fine sand or crushed particles of stone, mica or silica.

Oil-based Tough, hard-wearing paint that has oil as the binder and contains alkyd or polyurethane additives to increase the paint's durability.

Oil paint, which can usually be thinned with white spirit, is suitable for both indoor and outdoor surfaces, and is available with

a glossy, matt, mid-sheen or egg-shell finish.

Polyurethane An oil-based paint that has a
synthetic resin additive to improve its hard-
wearing properties.

Thixotropic A gelatinous, non-drip paint,
available in oil-based, vinyl and emulsions.
It must not be stirred.

PAINT BRUSHES The best paint
brushes (and often the most expensive) are
those made with pure grade natural bristle,
such as pig or boar. Each bristle, or fila-
ment, is tapered, which helps the brush to
keep its shape, has a rough surface for
paint to cling to, and has a split end, or
'flag', which helps the painter to get a
smooth and even finish.

The best synthetic 'bristle' is nylon; it is
cheaper than bristle but lasts longer. Nylon
may be used on its own in a brush, or in
combination with other synthetic materials
and natural bristles.

For painting walls and ceilings use a
150 mm or 100 mm (6 in. or 4 in.) wide
brush, and 75 mm, 50 mm, 25 mm and
12 mm (3 in., 2 in., 1 in. and ½ in.) brushes
for general house-painting jobs.

Other useful brushes are:
Cutting-in tool (Also known as a bevelled
tool). The tip of the brush is cut at a slant
to facilitate painting window GLAZING
BARS. Size: 19 mm (¾ in.).

Fitch Small, round-section brushes, used
for painting fine detail or narrow recessed
surfaces.

Sizes from 3 mm to 19 mm (⅛ in. to
¾ in.) diameter.

Radiator (crevice) A brush which has an
extra long metal handle for getting into
awkward areas, such as behind pipes and
radiators.

Sizes from 50 mm to 100 mm (2 ins. to
4 ins.).

Signwriting Small, thin paint brushes, used

for fine work, such as sign-writing or graining.

The best have squirrel or sable hairs.

Stippling A brush resembling a scrubbing brush with a handle on the back, used for texturing wet paint to achieve a stippled finish. Size 100 mm by 75 mm (4 ins. by 3 ins.).

PAINT KETTLE A cylindrical, lidless container with a handle, used for carrying small quantities of paint when working on a ladder.

They are made of polythene or galvanized iron, and are available from 125 mm to 200 mm (5 ins. to 8 ins.) diameter.

PAINT PAD A plastic holder with a replaceable rectangle of plastic foam, with a base surface of mohair bristles, used for applying paint.

Pad sizes from 50 mm by 25 mm (2 ins. by 1 in.) to 200 mm by 90 mm (8 ins. by 3½ ins.).

PAINT ROLLER A metal frame, with a handle, to which different cylinders or sleeves of material can be fixed in order to apply paint over a large area, e.g. walls and ceilings.

Materials available are: mohair, lambswool, foam and synthetic fibre. Mohair (short-pile) and man-made fibre are suitable for oil paint – both gloss and eggshell finishes; lambswool for emulsion paint – short-pile for smooth surfaces, and long-pile for rough; and foam rubber for all purposes, although this wears out quicker than the other materials.

Roller sizes are from 175 mm to 330 mm (approximately 7 ins. to 13 ins.) long.

PAINT SCRAPERS Knives with steel blades – from 25 mm to 125 mm (1 in. to 5 ins.) wide – used to scrape off softened paint or wallpaper.

The narrow scraper is useful for work on window frames, in conjunction with

SHAVEHOOKS, and can also double as a putty knife.

PAINT STRIPPER Proprietary fluids that can be applied to the surface of existing paintwork or varnish in order to soften it and make it easier to strip off.

PAINT TRAY A metal tray, with a sloping bottom, for holding paint when using a paint roller. The bottom of the tray has a corrugated surface so that the roller can be pressed down and surplus paint squeezed out.

PANEL HEATER ♦ HEATERS

PANEL PIN ♦ NAILS

PANELLED DOOR A door consisting of a framework of vertical and horizontal timbers, with infill panels of wood or glass.

Panelled doors were originally designed to minimize the movement that occurs when the moisture in wood dries out. Nowadays, with the more stabilized manmade boards available, such as plywood and blockboard, panelled doors are valued chiefly for their aesthetic qualities. (♦ DOORS)

PANEL SAW ♦ SAWS

PANTILES S-shape clay tiles. On a pantile roof, each tile overlaps a tile on one side, and is overlapped by a tile on the other; and each row of tiles is overlapped by the row above it.

PAPERHANGER'S TABLE A folding table that is ideal for pasting wallpaper. A common size is 1800 mm by 600 mm (6 ft by 2 ft).

PARAPET GUTTER A BOX GUTTER, formed IN SITU between a roof and a parapet wall. The gutter may be lined with zinc, copper, lead or asphalt.

PARLIAMENT HINGE ♦ HINGES

PARQUET FLOORING ♦ WOOD-BLOCK FLOORING

PARTIAL CENTRAL HEATING ♦ CENTRAL HEATING

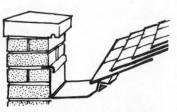

parapet gutter

PARTICLE BOARD An alternative name sometimes used for CHIPBOARD.

PARTING BEADS Thin strips of wood on a DOUBLE-HUNG SASH WINDOW that separate the inner and outer sashes and create a groove for them to slide up and down in.

PARTING SLIP A long narrow strip of wood in the side of a SASH WINDOW, which separates the counterbalance weights and prevent them from colliding when the sashes are raised and lowered.

Also known as a wagtail.

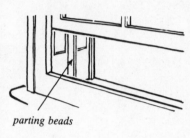

parting beads

PARTY WALL The dividing wall between two terraced or semi-detached houses, that is usually divided in ownership.

Also known as a partition wall.

PASTING BRUSH ◆ WALLPAPERING BRUSH

PATENT GLAZING The term applied to any form of glazing that uses a system of channels, grooves and metal clips – rather than conventional PUTTY and SPRIGS – to make a weatherproof window or glass roof.

PATINA The protective film that forms on metals when they are exposed to the air, due to the effects of oxidization. The familiar green colour that copper acquires is a typical example. Patinas can be artificially accelerated with chemicals but are not always aesthetically successful.

PATTERNED GLASS ◆ GLASS

PATTERN STAINING a characteristic fault that sometimes occurs in an uninsulated ceiling.

As warm air rises, it takes dirt in the air to the coldest surfaces, namely the plasterboard ceiling, where it clings. It does not cling however to the parts of the ceiling directly beneath the joists – wood is a good insulator – and as a result the lines of the joists can be seen from below, showing white against the stained ceiling.

PAVERS Specially-made bricks that are hard, dense, frost-resistant and often textured to provide non-slip surfaces for pedestrian areas.

They are usually the same length and breadth as bricks but only 50 mm (2 ins.) thick.

(◆ BRICKS)

PEBBLEDASH A textured finish applied to the outside of BRICK or BUILDING BLOCK walls, to improve their weathering characteristics, as well as their appearance. Small, clean pebbles and/or crushed stone – graded from 6 mm to 12 mm ($\frac{1}{4}$ in. to $\frac{1}{2}$ in.) – are literally thrown on to the second coat of a freshly-RENDERED SAND-and-CEMENT WALL.

PELLETING Using DOWEL-shaped pieces of wood to conceal screw-heads in good class joinery work. The pellet is cut from matching timber and fitted so that the grain of both the workpiece and the pellet are in line.

PELMET A decorative board or curtain fixed to the head of a window, or to a low ceiling, to conceal the curtain fittings. It may also conceal an electric light tube for indirect lighting.

PERPENDS The vertical joints in brickwork or blockwork. To 'keep the perpends' is to build the brickwork accurately, so that all the perpends line up with the courses above and below.

PETROL INTERCEPTOR A surface water TRAP that separates any petrol or oil from rainwater, or surface waste water, before it enters the sewers. The trap is sectionalized in such a way as to allow the volatile materials to evaporate.

Petrol interceptors are often necessary for draining hardstanding areas, flanked by private garages.

PHILLIPS SCREWDRIVER ◆ SCREWDRIVERS

PIANO HINGE ◆ HINGES

111

PIERCING SAW ♦ SAWS

PICTURE RAIL A moulded strip of wood on the walls of a room, usually coinciding with the top of the door height, for hanging pictures. Little used in modern houses, they are still commonplace in pre-war properties.

PIGMENT ♦ PAINT

PILES ♦ FOUNDATIONS

PILLAR TAP ♦ TAPS

PILOT HOLE A starter hole, of a slightly smaller diameter, that is drilled in timber before driving home a screw. It ensures accurate positioning and can help to prevent the wood splitting.

PILOT LIGHT A small gas flame that burns continuously on some kinds of INSTANTANEOUS WATER HEATERS, cooker rings, refrigerators and central heating BOILERS, to ignite the appliance when switched on.

PINCERS A gripping tool designed for pulling out nails from wood. One of the handles has its end shaped like a claw, used for levering up bent nails or removing tacks.

Sizes from 150 mm to 250 mm (6 ins. to 10 ins.).

PIN PUSH A spring-loaded tool used for 'pushing' home small nails or pins. Its magnetized barrel makes it an easier tool to use, in some cases, than a hammer.

PITCHED ROOF A sloping roof – whether with two slopes or one.

PIPE BENDER ♦ BENDING SPRING

PIPE WRENCH ♦ WRENCHES

PIVOT HINGE ♦ HINGES

PLAIN TILES Clay or concrete roofing tiles – originally handmade but now largely machine-made – with two small nibs (or projections) at one end to hook over TILING BATTENS, and two 6 mm ($\frac{1}{4}$ in.) diameter nail holes.

Plain tiles are 265 mm by 165 mm (10$\frac{1}{2}$ ins. by 6$\frac{1}{2}$ ins.) wide and 10 mm to

15 mm ($\frac{3}{8}$ in. to $\frac{5}{8}$ in.) thick.

Although known as flat tiles they have a slight camber to help resist the effects of CAPILLARY ACTION in wet weather.

PLANED-ALL-ROUND (PAR) Prepared SOFTWOOD that has been planed on all surfaces and is therefore about 3 mm ($\frac{1}{8}$ in.) smaller than the NOMINAL SIZE.

PLANES Sophisticated tools with a cutting edge for smoothing and shaping wood. A selection of the many different types is as follows:

Block For trimming END GRAIN timber. Lengths from 90 mm to 205 mm (approximately 3$\frac{1}{2}$ ins. to 8 ins.).

Bull nose For planing up the edge of a vertical surface. Lengths from 75 mm to 115 mm (3 ins. to 4$\frac{1}{2}$ ins.).

Jack A good, general purpose plane, but chiefly used on the bench for the preliminary planing of rough timber. Jack planes may be metal or wood. Lengths of metal planes are from 355 mm to 380 mm (14 ins. to 15 ins.), and wooden planes from 355 mm to 455 mm (14 ins. to 18 ins.).

Moulding A plane with a blade ground to cut concave or convex mouldings in timber. Different types are available to cut different shapes. Length 237 mm (about 9$\frac{1}{2}$ ins.).

Rebate A plane for cutting rebates (recesses) in timber. The essential difference is that the cutting edge of the blade is as wide as the plane. Lengths from 230 mm to 330 mm (9 ins. to 13 ins.).

Shoulder A variety of shoulder planes is available, used for trimming up rebates and cutting across end grain timber. Sizes vary in thickness from 15 mm to 31 mm ($\frac{5}{8}$ in. to 1$\frac{1}{4}$ ins.).

Spokeshave A two-handled metal plane for shaping and smoothing curved narrow sections of wood. There are two types of spokeshave: those with curved or convex

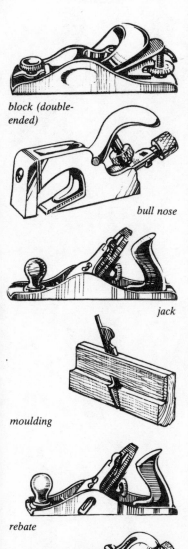

block (double-ended)

bull nose

jack

moulding

rebate

shoulder

113

blades for cutting concave shapes; and those with flat or concave blades to cut flat or concave shapes.

Sizes of blade widths vary from 43 mm to 53 mm (1¾ in. to 2⅛ ins.).

PLANNING PERMISSION A legal requirement that governs how land and buildings are used.

Unlike the BUILDING REGULATIONS, which are primarily framed to make buildings safe, planning permission deals with the appearance of an individual building and its relation to neighbouring properties.

Local planning authorities provide application forms and details outlining their requirements.

Failure to comply with the regulations can mean having to restore the work to its original state.

PLANTED STOP The thin strip of timber nailed to the inside face of a DOOR LINING, to provide a surface for the door to stop against.

PLASTER Material applied to walls and ceilings in a plastic state to provide, when it dries, a hard smooth or textured surface for decoration. Different types of plaster have different characteristics, chiefly in their setting times, with some drying quickly and therefore ideal for small areas of repair work, and others drying slowly and easier to use when plastering large areas.

Applications vary from one to three coats, according to the quality of finish required.

PLASTERBOARD A man-made board consisting of a plaster core sandwiched between two sheets of heavy paper – one cream-coloured, the other grey.

Plasterboard is generally used for ceilings and lining timber framed partitions – either fixed dry with the cream-coloured paper facing outwards for decorations or, more commonly, with the grey side outwards and surfaced with a skim coat of

PLASTER, about 3 mm (⅛ in.) thick.

Specially insulated plasterboard has a backing of aluminium foil. Other specialized boards are also available.

Sheets vary in size but are generally available in 2440 mm by 1220 mm (8 ft by 4 ft) wide, and 9.5 mm and 12.7 mm (⅜ in. and ½ in.) thick.

PLASTER OF PARIS A hemi-hydrate plaster, i.e. one that sets rapidly once it has been mixed with water. Since it dries within ten minutes or so, it is ideal if a casting is needed, such as when repairing broken mouldings on a valued picture frame.

PLASTIC LAMINATE ♦ LAMINATED PLASTIC

PLASTIC FLOORING There are two basic types of flooring material: asbestos vinyl and flexible vinyl – both consisting of a blend of plastic resins with fillers.

Asbestos vinyl This is the least flexible of the two (it has more asbestos filler in it) and the floor it is laid on does not have to have a DPC, although it is preferable. Asbestos vinyl is only available in tile form – commonly 300 mm by 300 mm by 2 mm (12 ins. by 12 ins. by $\frac{1}{16}$ in.) thick.

Flexible vinyl This is the more expensive of the two plastic materials; it is manufactured in both sheet and tile form, and is available in a large range of colours. It may be solid vinyl, i.e. the same thickness of wearing material throughout or, more commonly, consist of a top wearing layer, which contains the colour, bonded to an uncoloured base material.

Printed vinyls have a thin layer of transparent vinyl covering.

There are also alternative backing materials for these vinyls (felt or foam-rubber) which help deaden the impact sounds of shoes etc.

PLASTICIZER A proprietary material that can be added to mortar or concrete to make it easier to work.

PLASTIC WOOD A proprietary paste that can be used to fill small nail holes or indentations in wood. Plastic wood is made in different colours to match different types of wood, such as oak, walnut or mahogany.

A highly volatile material, it dries rapidly and when hard can be cut with a chisel, smoothed with ABRASIVES or painted.

PLATE GLASS ♦ GLASS

PLIERS Gripping tools for manipulating metal and wire. They should not be used, however, instead of spanners, or the pliers will damage the corners of nuts.

A selection from the many different types is:

Engineer's The essential all-round, general purpose pliers. They have serrated jaws for gripping things, a rod-gripping section, side-cutters for snipping wire. Sizes from 125 mm to 250 mm (5 ins. to 10 ins.).

Electrician's The same as engineer's pliers but with the handles fitted, during manufacture, with sleeves of insulation material.

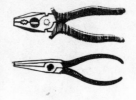

Flat nose Pliers with long, narrow jaws and no cutting edges, but flat, serrated meeting surfaces. Useful for working on lightweight metals and wire. Sizes from 100 mm to 187 mm (4 ins. to $7\frac{3}{8}$ ins.).

Slip joint Pliers with jaws that are pivoted with a joint that can be engaged in an alternative position to open wider still. This second position offers less gripping strength but much more potential for working with plumbing pipework.

Sizes from 125 mm to 250 mm (5 ins. to 10 ins.).

Snipe-nosed Pliers with long taper jaws that are useful for more delicate work, such as handling small electrical fittings. Sizes from 112 mm to 200 mm (roughly $4\frac{1}{2}$ ins. to 8 ins.).

Wire strippers Pliers which have angled jaws with V-shaped cuts in them. When the jaws are closed over a length of electric

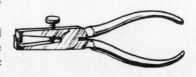

cable, they bite into the insulation, which can then be stripped off.

Sizes from 150 mm to 200 mm (6 ins. to 8 ins.).

PLUG An insulated fitting that enables an electric appliance to be connected to a SOCKET OUTLET.

Also describes a small cylinder of wood, fibre, metal, nylon or plastic, that is inserted into a wall to provide a fixing for screws.

(◆ WALL PLUGS)

PLUG CUTTER ◆ BITS

PLUMB BOB AND LINE A pointed weight, made of metal or plastic, attached to a nylon or silk line, used to establish the vertical, when, for example, wallpapering or fixing a door frame.

PLUMBER The tradesman who instals all water pipework in a house, i.e. cuts, bends and joins all water and waste pipes, and the associated fittings, such as bath, basins, sinks, etc.

The plumber is also the tradesmen who fixes metal roof covering, such as zinc or lead.

PLUNGER A useful tool that will often free a blockage in a water closet or basin. It has a rubber cup, on the end of a wooden handle, that is placed over the outlet of a basin or sink, or in the bowl of a water closet, and 'pumped' to create surges of pressure.

Sizes from 62 mm to 125 mm (2½ ins. to 5 ins.) diameter.

PLYWOOD A manufactured board consisting of an odd number of veneers, bonded together under pressure to make strong and stable material. An odd number is used to prevent warping and the grain of each veneer is laid at right angles to adjacent veneers for additional strength.

Plywood marked 'Exterior WBP' (weather and boil-proof) is manufactured with waterproof adhesive and is suitable for external use.

Plywood is made with various decorative finishes, such as plastic or metal laminate, as well as various types of hardwood veneer finish.

It is made in various thicknesses, from 3 mm to 19 mm ($\frac{1}{8}$ in. to $\frac{3}{4}$ in.) and is commonly available in 1220 mm (4 ft) square sheets. Other sizes are also made.

POCKET SCREWING ◆ SECRET SCREWING

POINTINGThe method of finishing the joints between brick COURSES using a different mortar from that used to lay the bricks.

As the bricks are laid, the joints are raked out to a depth of 19 mm ($\frac{3}{4}$ in.). When the brickwork is finished, the recesses are then filled with a CEMENT MORTAR in any one of several ways: flush, hollow, keyed (or recessed), or weathered. A masonry joint is used for stonework.

Pointing makes it easier to ensure the colour of the mortar in a large area of brickwork will look the same when finished. It also provides an opportunity for a colouring additive to be used if contrasting effects are wanted.

(◆ JOINTING)

POINTING TROWEL ◆ TROWELS

POLYURETHANE PAINT ◆ PAINT

POLYURETHANE VARNISH A varnish that can be applied by brush or spray to seal woodwork and give it a hard, protective finish that is easy to maintain and is resistant to heat, water and sunlight.

Different grades are made for interior and exterior use. In addition to colourless polyurethane, some manufacturers supply a limited range of transparent colours, which allow the grain and character of the wood to show through. Finishes available are gloss, satin and matt.

Polyurethane varnish is sold in one-pack form, i.e. ready for use, but some two-pack

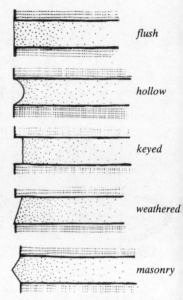

flush

hollow

keyed

weathered

masonry

varieties are also available – suitable where extremely hard-wearing properties are needed. The two-pack form, in separate tins, contains a lacquer and a catalyst, which must be mixed before application.

POLYVINYLCHLORIDE (PVC) A tough and durable form of plastic which is used for many floor coverings, rainwater pipes and gutters, and some plumbing pipework.

PORTLAND CEMENT The most commonly used *cement* – so-called because when dry it resembles PORTLAND STONE.

PORTLAND STONE An attractive and hard-wearing limestone from Portland in Dorset, mostly used as a facing material to brickwork.

POWER DRILL ♦ DRILLS

POWER TOOL ATTACHMENTS In addition to the large range of BITS that can be fitted to an electric power tool, there are various other attachments useful for diverse jobs about the house.

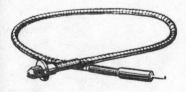

Flexible drive An invaluable accessory that enables the drive to be transmitted from a power tool, through a spiral cable encased by a flexible steel liner, to an attachment, such as a polishing pad. The flexible drive makes some attachments easier to use and is also easier for getting into awkward or constricted spaces.

Size from 750 mm to 1300 mm (29½ ins. to roughly 51 ins.) long.

Polishing pad A lambswool bonnet that can be tied over a rubber backing pad for polishing wood or metal.

Rubber backing pad A tough rubber disc, that can be fitted to a power tool with a threaded shaft, as a backing surface when using sanding discs.

Sanding discs Paper or metal discs with abrasive material bonded to one side, which are used for sanding wood, metal or plastics. Abrasive textures vary from fine to extra coarse.

119

Sizes from 100 mm to 225 mm (4 ins. to 9 ins.) diameters.

Wire brushes Ideal for removing rust from metal or for cleaning brickwork. A wire brush wheel is suitable for attaching to a power tool directly, or a wire-cup brush to a flexible drive.

(♦ SANDING MACHINES; SAWS)

POZIDRIVE SCREWDRIVER ♦ SCREWDRIVERS

PRECAST CONCRETE Concrete cast in specific shapes, such as thresholds, lintels, fireplace throats, etc. Precast concrete items can often be bought from builders' merchants.

PRE-PASTED PAPER ♦ WALL-PAPERS

PRESERVATIVES Fluids such as paint, chemical insecticides, water repellents and fungicides that can be applied to timber to protect it from decay. Metals, which can also be protected with paint, often have a protective finish given to them during manufacture to prevent rusting, such as SHERARDIZING, cadmium plating, or phosphating.

PRESSED STEEL LINTEL ♦ LINTELS

PRE-STRESSED CONCRETE Concrete reinforced with high tensile prestressed wires instead of the more usual mild steel rods used in REINFORCED CONCRETE.

Prestressed concrete LINTELS are therefore lighter and thinner than conventional lintels – often no deeper than a brick COURSE.

PRIMARY CIRCUIT The pipework through which water flows from a BOILER to HOT WATER CYLINDER and back to the boiler again. The pipes are known respectively as the flow and return pipes.

PRIMER ♦ PAINT

PROFILE BOARDS Temporary erections on site, used with string to set out the line of the FOUNDATIONS of a building.

PROGRAMMER A 24 hour time clock that can be set to control CENTRAL HEATING and hot water requirements. Programmers vary from relatively simple types, offering the choice of five alternative settings, to the more sophisticated models governing sixteen different programmes.

PTFE TAPE A plastic – polytetrafluorethylene – tape, used to seal joints in water pipes.

The white tape is wrapped around the male half of a connector, before being screwed into the female half.

P-TRAP ♦ TRAPS

PUGGING Material placed between the joists in a SUSPENDED WOODEN FLOOR in order to help deaden the transmission of sounds.

(♦ INSULATION MATERIALS)

PULL-CORD SWITCH ♦ SWITCH

PULLEY STILE The sides of a SASH WINDOW that have the pulley wheels – over which the cords attached to the counterbalance weights pass.

PUNCHES ♦ CENTRE PUNCH; NAIL PUNCH; SOLID PUNCH

PURLIN The heavy section of timber spanning the structural walls in a roof, to provide support at or near the centre of the main RAFTERS.

PUSH-DRILL ♦ DRILLS

PUTTY A plastic material – a mixture of whiting and linseed oil – that is pliable until it is exposed to the air, when it starts to set hard. Putty is used by glaziers for bedding and waterproofing glass in window-frames, and for filling blemishes in woodwork, before painting it.

PUTTY KNIFE A knife with a flexible steel blade used to apply putty when glazing windows. There are several types of

putty knife, with different shaped blades,
e.g. pointed, curved or straight.

Blade widths vary from 38 mm to 50 mm
($1\frac{1}{2}$ ins. to 2 ins.).

PVA ADHESIVE ◗ ADHESIVES

PVC ◗ POLYVINYLCHLORIDE

Q

QUARREL A pane of glass in a LEADED LIGHT.

QUARRIES ◆ QUARRY TILES

QUARRY TILES Square clay paving tiles – also known as quarries – usually red, but sometimes black or brown, with a hard dense surface and little porosity.

Old quarries can be sometimes be found up to 300 mm (12 ins.) square and 38 mm (1½ ins.) thick; but nowadays the common size is generally 150 mm (6 ins.) square and 19 mm (¾ in.) thick.

QUEEN CLOSER ◆ CLOSER

QUILT ◆ INSULATION MATERIALS

QUIRK A narrow V-shaped groove or recess between two adjacent MOULDINGS.

QUOIN The outer corner of a building or a wall. Quoins are also the large corner stones used on buildings which have the remainder of the walls built of brick, flint or rubble masonry.

A squint quoin is where the external corner is more or less than a right angle.

RACKING BACK A method of building a new wall so that the brickwork is about twelve courses higher at the ends than it is at the centre, each course stepped back a minimum of about 57 mm (2¼ ins.).

Racking back helps to spread the load evenly on a foundation and avoids the possibility of settlement cracks appearing when the rest of the wall is built.

RADIAL ARM SAW ♦ SAWS

RADIAL CIRCUIT A form of wiring for domestic socket outlets. Unlike a ring circuit, only one CABLE is connected to the consumer unit and this may supply up to six socket outlets, depending upon their location and fuse rating.

Radial circuits were originally used for round-pin sockets but were re-introduced some time after the RING CIRCUIT was devised.

RADIANT CONVECTOR HEATER ♦ HEATERS

RADIANT HEATER ♦ HEATERS

RAFTERS The principle structural timbers on a pitched roof or a flat roof. Also known as spars.

RAG BOLT ♦ ANCHOR BOLT

RAINWATER HOPPER ♦ GUTTERS AND DOWNPIPES

RAINWATER PIPES ♦ GUTTERS AND DOWNPIPES

RAISED-HEAD SCREW ♦ SCREWS

RAKED JOINT Joints in old brickwork may be raked out with a cold chisel to a depth of about 19 mm (¾ in.) in order to provide a key for a covering material, such as RENDERING or ROUGH CAST.

RASPS Shaping tools that are similar to FILES but suitable for rougher preparatory work, and for working on soft metals, such as aluminium.

Flat, round and half-round shapes are available with bastard (coarse) and smooth cutting surfaces.

A proprietary shaping tool in this category is the Surform – a rasp consisting of a flat or round replaceable blade – perforated with a series of sharp-edged holes.

Sizes of conventional rasps vary from 150 mm to 400 mm (6 ins. to 16 ins.) long; Surforms 250 mm (10 ins.).

RATCHET BRACE ♦ DRILLS

RATCHET SCREWDRIVER ♦ SCREWDRIVERS

RAT-TRAP BOND ♦ BONDS

READY-MIXED CONCRETE Freshly mixed concrete, still in its fluid state, which is delivered to the site by lorry ready to be laid IN SITU.

Ready-mix – for quantities up to $2\frac{1}{2}$ m³ (3 yds³) – can be a considerable advantage to the handyman, providing all preparatory work has been done beforehand and that there are sufficient helpers to spread the material quickly: within an hour or two of delivery.

READY-PASTED WALLPAPER ♦ WALLPAPER

READY-TRIMMED WALLPAPER ♦ WALLPAPER

REBATE A rectangular recess cut in the edge of a piece of wood, either as part of a joint or to receive the edge of a panel, door or similar construction.

Also known as a rabbet.

REBATE PLANE ♦ PLANES

RECESSED-HEAD SCREW ♦ SCREWS

RECESSED JOINTING ♦ POINTING

REINFORCED BUTT JOINT ♦ END-TO-END JOINT

REINFORCED CONCRETE CON-CRETE strengthened with mild steel rods or mesh so that it has a tensile strength comparable with its natural compressive strength. The position of reinforcing material is critical – found by calculating the stresses and strains that will be imposed upon it by a particular workload.

(◗ PRE-STRESSED CONCRETE)

RELIEF PAPER ◗ WALLPAPERS

RENDERING The first covering coat of sharp sand and cement applied to a brick or concrete block wall, before covering it internally with PLASTER, or, externally, with sand, LIME and cement.

Rendering conceals any irregularities in the surface and provides a relatively smooth surface for the 'finishing' coat. Sometimes a second, intermediate coat is used, known as a 'floating' coat.

Render and set (which is two-coat work) has a first coat between 10 mm and 13 mm ($\frac{3}{8}$ in. and $\frac{1}{2}$ in.) thick and a finishing coat of 3 mm ($\frac{1}{8}$ in.).

Render, float and set (which is three-coat work) has first and second coats about 3 mm ($\frac{1}{8}$ in.) thick.

REPAIR GRANTS ◗ GRANTS

RESIN-BONDED Materials that are resin-bonded, for example, external quality PLYWOOD, are glued with synthetic resins and are therefore moisture resistant.

RETAINING WALL A brick or concrete wall that supports, or retains, earth at a higher level on one side of the wall than the other.

RETURNED END The corner of a brick wall, whatever its angle.

RETURN MOULDING The end of a moulding which is finished with a shape that matches its own profile.

REVEAL The sides of a door or window opening in a wall that are not covered by the framework or the linings.

RIDGE The apex of a pitched (sloping) roof.

RIDGE TILE A purpose-made and specially shaped tile that is bedded in mortar to cover and weatherproof the RIDGE on a roof.

The ridge tiles are made in various materials to match the roof coverings, such as clay and concrete tiles, slate, asbestos cement, and metal.

RIM LATCH ♦ LOCKS AND LATCHES

RIM LOCK ♦ LOCKS AND LATCHES

RING CIRCUIT A system of wiring, introduced in Britain in 1947, using only 13 amp sockets to receive flat, three-pin plugs. The plugs have their own fuses and can therefore be fused to match the rating of the appliances they are wired to.

More commonly – but less accurately referred to as a 'ring main' – each ring circuit runs from the fuse board to serve one or more floors and back to the fuse board. Each circuit can serve a maximum of 100 sq. m (about 1000 sq ft) of floor space and a maximum of 7200 watts (7.2 kW) – protected at the fuse board by a 30 amp fuse.

Provided these limitations are not exceeded, it may also have any number of socket outlets.

RING MAIN ♦ RING CIRCUIT

RIP SAW ♦ SAWS

RISERS The vertical faces of a step.

RISING BUTTS ♦ HINGES

RISING DAMP Moisture that rises up through the structure (due to CAPILLARY ACTION) from those parts of the house in contact with the soil. Rising damp occurs in houses where there is no DAMP-PROOF COURSE, or the existing one has deteriorated. It manifests itself first at skirting level and often rises in a band of discolouration and dampness for a height of about a metre (a yard), with peeling wallpaper, staining and EFFLORESCENCE.

127

RISING MAIN A gas, water, or electricity supply pipe or cable that comes from the respective authorities' mains in the road to serve a house.

RODDING EYE An opening in a soil, waste or rainwater pipe – usually on a bend – that is sealed with a small access plate. This can be removed if a blockage occurs and rodded through with drainage equipment.

Also known as an access eye.

(◆ DRAIN RODS)

ROLLED STEEL JOIST (RSJ) An H- or L-shaped steel beam, available in various standard sizes and thicknesses.

ROOF COVERINGS ◆ ASPHALT; BITUMINOUS FELT; ITALIAN TILING; PLAIN TILING; SPANISH TILING; SHINGLES; SLATES; STONE SLATES

ROOFING FELT A bituminous felt, used on a roof between the rafters and the covering materials, such as slates or tiles, to keep the attic space free of dust and to assist, marginally, with heat insulation.

Also known as sarking felt.

ROOF LIGHT A window in a roof, such as a skylight or DORMER.

ROSE ◆ CEILING ROSE

ROUGH BRACKETS SOFTWOOD boards, 25 mm (1 in.) thick, nailed alternately to the sides of the CARRIAGE PIECE beneath a staircase, to provide additional support for the TREADS.

ROUGHCAST An external wall finish – also known as spar dash – used to improve both the appearance and weathering properties of a wall.

Roughcast consists of a cement, sand and lime RENDERING, with pea gravel, marble or granite chippings, thrown – or dashed – on to the rendering while it is still plastic.

ROUND-HEAD SCREW ◆ SCREWS

ROUTER A metal tool, similar to a PLANE, used for cutting grooves in timber

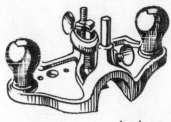

hand router

surfaces. There are several types of router made, including a power-driven one which can be fitted with scores of different types of cutting BITS.

The hand router is usually available with three cutters: a 6 mm and 12 mm (¼ in. and ½ in.) wide chisels, and a V-shaped cutter.

RUBBER ◆ BRICKS

RUBBED-BRICK ◆ BRICKS

RUBBED JOINT A glued joint in wood-work, used to join two boards edge to edge. The meeting faces are planed smooth, adhesive is applied to them and they are then rubbed together under pres-sure, until all surplus adhesive is squeezed out and air expelled.

The surplus is wiped off and the boards clamped together until the adhesive has set, to form a strong joint.

Also a flush joint used in brickwork.

RUBBING DOWN Cleaning and pre-paring painted surfaces for redecoration.

RUBBLE WALLING Stones that are roughly cut to shape, but not necessarily squared, and used for building stone walls. There are various kinds of rubble walling: random rubble laid without COURSES; coursed random rubble, laid with courses from 300 mm to 450 mm (12 ins. to 18 ins.) wide, according to the size of stones available; and squared rubble, which has the largest stones squared up as neatly as possible and bonded with smaller stones laid to courses.

RULES Many different types of measur-ing rules are available, but two or three of these will be sufficient for most jobs en-countered in household DIY.

Most rules nowadays are manufactured with metric or imperial graduations, or a combination of both. Wherever possible select the rule that combines both.

Folding rules These are convenient to handle and carry and a boon when working in a confined space.

129

The traditional four-fold or 'carpenter's' rule is 610 mm (24 ins.) long. It is both pivoted and hinged so that it can be folded into a quarter of its length.

A single-folding rule, of the same length, folds in half only.

A zigzag rule – up to 2 m (roughly 6 ft 6 ins.) long – is pivoted at every 330 mm (13 ins.) or 165 mm (6½ ins.) of its length and folds up when not in use.

Folding rules are made in boxwood, metal or plastic, and in combinations of all three materials.

Bench rule A straight, hardwood rule, available up to 2 m (roughly 6 ft 6 ins.) long.

Steel rule An essential when setting out accurate dimensions on metal work, as well as being a useful straight edge. Lengths vary from 150 mm to 2 m (6 ins. to roughly 6 ft 6 ins.).

Steel tape Also known as a flexible rule, or push-pull tape, this is a spring-loaded rule that is coiled inside its casing. The tape can be withdrawn and either stays in position wherever necessary until it is pushed back, or it can be locked in position. Once unlocked the tape springs back into the case.

Tapes are available in lengths from 900 mm to 5 m (roughly 3 ft to 16 ft) in plastic or metal cases.

RUSTIC ◆ BRICKS

SABRE SAW ◆ SAWS
SACRIFICIAL ANODE ◆ ELECTRO-
LYTIC ACTION
SADDLEBACK STONE ◆ COPING
SAND Minute particles of siliceous stone,
used with CEMENT to make MORTAR or,
with the addition of AGGREGATE to make
CONCRETE.

Sand provides bulk, adhesion, reduces
shrinkage and ensures a mixture is adequately aerated.

Soft builders' sand is used for bricklaying
and plastering; sharp sand – which is
slightly larger and grittier – for concrete
where a greater strength is required.

Silver sand, which is suitable for children's play pits, does not stain clothing.
SAND-FACED BRICK ◆ BRICKS
SANDING BLOCK A convenient hand-
size block of hard material around which
abrasive paper is wrapped or secured, for
use when sanding wood smooth.

Blocks are available made of wood, plastic, cork, or a dense rubber.
SANDING MACHINES Power-driven
machines – both big and small – that are
fitted with abrasive materials for sanding
wood surfaces smooth.
Flooring sanders These are powerful
machines that will sand a floor surface
quickly and with relatively little mess, since
they are fitted with dustbags – like vacuum
cleaners – and can easily be removed and
emptied. See left.

Both types can be hired from plant hire
specialists.
Drum sander This is the larger of the

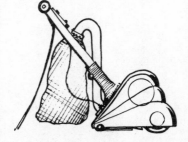

two – of lawn-mower proportions – and is suitable for sanding the main area of a floor. It is fitted with sheets of abrasive material that wrap around a revolving drum.

Rotary sander Useful for finishing off the edges of a floor after a drum sander has been used.

The following two machines are power-tool attachments:

Foam drum sander A 125 mm (5 ins.) diameter drum, with a steel shaft in the centre for fixing to the power tool chuck. An endless belt of abrasive paper is slipped over the drum, which is slightly resilient and therefore suitable for sanding curved as well as flat surfaces.

Orbital sander Useful for giving a final sheen to a surface that has already been sanded. Strips of abrasive paper are fitted to the base pad – 100 mm (4 ins.) square – which operate in small circular movements. Some machines have an alternative switch position to make 'linear' movements.

rotary sander

orbital sander

SANDPAPER ♦ ABRASIVES

SARKING FELT ♦ ROOFING FELT

SASH A window whose opening portions slide up and down, counterbalanced by springs or weights on sash cords.

SASH BAR A vertical glazing bar in a window.

SASH CORD Plaited terylene cord, sold in builders' merchants specifically for supporting the weights in a sash window. Waxed and plaited cords are also available.

SASH CRAMP ♦ CRAMPS

SAUCER DOME A rooflight made of SAFETY GLASS or translucent plastic, which is shaped like an inverted saucer and supported on metal framing.

SAW HORSE A four-legged trestle sturdy enough to be used for supporting materials when sawing.

SAWS The right saw for the right job is an obvious advantage, but the range of types available is large and varied enough to be both unnecessary and too expensive for all but the dedicated purist. A study of the saws listed below will reveal that there are many saws capable of doing more than one job efficiently enough for the average handyman.

The size of a saw's teeth varies, and each saw is described as having so many points (teeth) to the 25 mm (1 in.). The greater the number of points the finer the cut. And the slower the cutting rate.

Backsaws A family of saws which have rectangular blades that are stiffened along the back, non-cutting edge with a strip of heavy brass or steel. The two types are the *tenon* saw and the *gent's* saw, both used primarily for cutting fine timber joints.

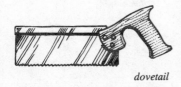

dovetail

The tenon (which is also known as the dovetail, because it is intended for cutting dovetail joints) is often the 'general-purpose' saw in an amateur's tool bag. It has 11 to 20 points per 25 mm.

The gent's saw (which is another saw known as a dovetail saw) has 15 to 21 points per 25 mm and is used for cutting finer joints than its companions.

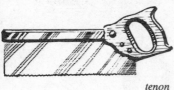

tenon

Coping A saw for cutting curves in wood. It has a narrow, fine-toothed – fourteen points per 25 mm – replaceable blade, which is held in place by the natural spring of the bow-shaped frame. The blade can cut at any angle but the depth of the cut is limited by the depth of the bow – 118 mm (about 4⅝ ins.).

The *fret saw* (or *piercing saw*) is similar in principle but has a deeper bow to the frame, and a finer cutting edge to the blades – thirty-two points per 25 mm.

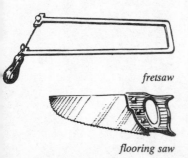

fretsaw

flooring saw

Flooring A saw with eight points per 25 mm and a cutting edge that is curved, in order to simplify sawing a floorboard without damaging the ones each side of it. Size is 312 mm (roughly 12 ins.) long.

Frame (or Bow) A saw with a replaceable

blade, held in a wooden frame, which is tensioned by twisting a cord and anchoring it with a wing nut or a wooden toggle. Used for cutting curves and 'heavy' work, such as cutting across the grain.

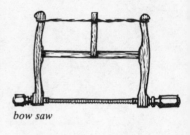

bow saw

Hacksaw An adjustable steel-framed saw for cutting metals. It will take blades 200 mm, 250 mm and 300 mm (8 ins., 10 ins. and 12 ins.) long.

Junior Hacksaw A fixed metal frame which is tensioned enough to hold the replaceable blades. Used for fine metal work, which a hacksaw would be too big for.

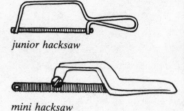

junior hacksaw

Mini Hacksaw A plastic handle with a screw clamp that can be fitted with hacksaw blades to make a handy supplementary saw to the hacksaw. Can be used for broken as well as new hacksaw blades.

mini hacksaw

Padsaw (also *Compass* or *Keyhole*) A saw to cut holes in panels – from keyhole size upwards. The handle has a locking screw and can be fitted with different types of blades: small, medium and large, with teeth ranging from fine to coarse. Blade lengths from 125 mm to 375 mm (roughly 5 ins. to 15 ins.) long.

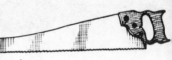

padsaw

Panel One of the amateur's essential saws – the other is the tenon. The panel saw has a long tapering blade – a useful length is 500 mm (20 ins.) with ten points per 25 mm – this is a good all-rounder, including cutting panels of man-made boards and planks. Choose one with a non-stick Teflon coating which helps to prevent the blade jamming in sappy timber. Also known as a cross-cut saw.

panel saw

Rip This is the 'big brother' to the panel saw, but has teeth which are five points per 25 mm. Intended for cutting along the grain, the rip saw will tear wood if used across the grain.

For the amateur, the panel saw serves both purposes adequately.

Band saw An endless steel belt, passing over two wheels, to provide a continuous cutting edge. Used to cut intricate shapes and curves, and large sections of timber.

Power-tool saws These are for the more sophisticated woodworker:

Circular A portable saw that can be attached to a power tool, and can be fitted with a wide range of circular saw blades, that range from fine metal cutting to heavy rip sawing jobs.

It is principally intended for cutting through heavy timber, such as BLOCK-BOARD or similar boards.

Suitable blade diameters are 125 mm or 187 mm (5 ins. or 7⅜ ins.).

Jig saw (or Sabre) Another power tool attachment that is also very versatile. It can be fitted with several different types of blade for cutting wood or metal, in straight lines or curved shapes. Its great advantage is that it can be used to cut holes in panels, once a starting hole has been drilled for the blade. See left.

Radial arm Perhaps the most sophisticated saw of all, intended for bench work and a multiplicity of jobs. It can be fitted with many attachments and can range from jobs such as cutting joints in timber to being used as a sanding machine to a power drill. Types vary in horsepower from 1.35 to 4.5.

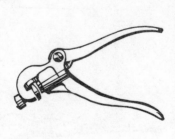

SAW SET A tool used to bend the teeth of a saw to the correct angle when the saw is being sharpened. See left.

SCAFFOLDING TOWER A sectional tower that can be erected by one man to provide a safe platform to work on, for instance, when painting a ceiling or doing roof repairs. The tower can be fitted with metal plates, for permanent erection, or on wheels – mobile enough for one man to move it. Plant hire firms and some DIY shops hire out towers on a weekly basis.

SCARF JOINT ◗ END-TO-END JOINTS
SCOTCH GLUE ◗ ADHESIVES
SCOTIA A hardwood moulding that resembles a concave quadrant.

SCRAPERS ♦ CABINET SCRAPER; SHAVE HOOKS; STRIPPING KNIFE

SCREED A layer of SAND and CEMENT – usually in the ratio of 4:1 or 3:1 – used in solid-floor construction to provide a smooth hard surface for floor-coverings, such as plastic or CORK TILING.

The thickness of a screed varies, but it must be sufficient to cover the irregularities in the concrete sub-floor and, if any, service CONDUITS. The average thickness is 50 mm (2 ins.).

SCREW CUPS AND WASHERS Raised or recessed metal washers that give an extra bite to make a firm joint when screwing into woodwork. Screw cups and washers present a neat appearance and can be an advantage on a workpiece that is to be dismantled from time to time.

SCREWDRIVERS Like most tools, good screwdrivers pay dividends provided they are used for the purpose they are intended and not as implements for levering or prising jobs.

To cope with the range of screw sizes one is likely to encounter in a home, three or four different sized screwdrivers are necessary. Most drivers have a flat blade for use with screws which have a single slot in their head – and a driver too large or too small is likely to damage a screw irreparably. For the same reason a Phillips or Pozidrive screwdriver (see below) is necessary for cross-shaped slotted screws.

Cabinet The woodworker's traditional driver, it has a steel blade and a large bulbous wooden handle that provides a good gripping surface. Blade lengths vary from 75 mm to 250 mm (3 ins. to 10 ins.).

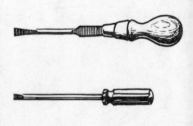

Electrician's A steel driver with a moulded plastic handle to make it safe to use. Some makes also have part of the blade's shaft insulated such as a mains tester, which incorporates a neon bulb – used to test for

the presence of an electrical current.

The driver – used on machine screws, such as those found in electrical fittings – is available with blade lengths varying from 75 mm to 250 mm (3 ins. to 10 ins.) long.

Phillips A steel driver with a pointed cross-shaped head (instead of the conventional shaped blade) designed for use only on screws with a matching cross-head indentation. The shape provides a more positive grip between driver and screw and lessens the likelihood of screw slots being damaged. It also has the advantage that a screw can be pushed on to the end of the driver – useful when working in an awkward space.

Blade lengths from 75 mm to 250 mm (3 ins. to 10 ins.). See left.

Pozidrive Similar to a Phillips driver but designed to fit an additional hole – square-shaped – in the middle of the cross-shaped slots in the screw heads.

Ratchet A driver with a steel blade that has a ratchet mechanism enabling the user to drive home screws (or unscrew them) without changing his grip on the handle. See left.

The ratchet can be operated by the thumb either to turn the driver clockwise or anti-clockwise, or remained fixed.

Blade lengths from 75 mm to 250 mm (3 ins. to 10 ins.).

Spiral ratchet Also known as a 'pump' or 'Yankee' screwdriver, this is similar to the ratchet driver except that the steel blade is linked to a spring-loaded spiral mechanism. When pressure is applied to the handle the blade turns and the spiral retracts into the hollow handle of the driver, automatically springing out again when pressure is released. A thumb-operated catch

137

can reverse the action of the driver or, as with the ratchet screwdriver, keep it in the fixed position. See above.

Blade lengths from 240 mm to 710 mm (9½ ins. to 28 ins.).

Stubby Short-bladed screwdrivers for use in constricted spaces.

Blade lengths are 25 mm and 38 mm (1 in. and 1½ ins.).

SCREWS All screws are classified by their gauge – the diameter of the shank – and their overall length, measured from screw head to the tip of the screw thread. Gauge numbers run from 1 to 20 – the lower the gauge the thinner the screw – and remain the same whatever the length of the screw. Thus, a 25 mm (1 in.) No. 8 screw and a 75 mm (3 in.) No. 8 screw have the same size head and diameter shank.

Screws are made in a variety of metals, aluminium, brass, copper, mild steel, etc., with a similar variety of finishes, e.g. galvanized, nickel-plated or black-japanned.

The common types in use are:

Countersunk A general purpose wood screw with a flat head which can be driven home to fit flush with the surface or slightly recessed, in order to conceal it with a FILLER.

Cross-head These have cross-shaped slots in the head and can only be used with a PHILLIPS or POZIDRIVE SCREWDRIVER. Like countersunk screws they fit flush with the surface.

Also known as recessed-head screws.

Dome-head Countersunk screws that have drilled heads to take the threaded shank of a covering dome, or a plastic snap-on dome. Dome-head screws are used for decorative work, such as fixing mirrors or panels.

Raised countersunk head A screw made primarily for fixing ironmongery fixtures, such as door handles or keyhole plates.

Used principally where a good standard of finish is required.

Round head Used for fixing one material to another where the first is too thin to be countersunk, e.g. PLYWOOD to framing.

Self-tapping Mild steel screws, with a hardened surface, designed to form or cut their own thread in (softer) metals as they are driven home. Used in metalwork, self-tapping screws are stronger than other types, and are available in a wide variety of head styles and gauges.

(♦ COACH SCREW)

SCRIBER A sharp, pointed steel tool, used for marking out metal.

SCRIBING A technique used to mark, cut and fit a material snugly against a vertical surface that is irregular, such as a worktop built against an uneven wall, or a skirting board against an uneven floor.

SEALANT ♦ MASTIC

SEALERS Fluids used to seal the surface of absorbent materials and give them a hard protective skin. Sealers may be transparent or opaque, and are often used on newly sanded wood floors.

(♦ VARNISH)

SEAM ROLLER A hardwood roller used to apply pressure to butt-joints between adjacent sheets of wall-covering materials, such as wallpaper or vinyl, to ensure they are firmly pasted down.

Roller widths – 25 mm and 50 mm (1 in. and 2 ins.).

SEASONING The drying of timber, artificially or naturally, to a specific MOISTURE CONTENT.

SECRET DOVETAILING ♦ DOVETAIL JOINT

SECRET GUTTER A gutter, usually formed IN SITU, that is screened by a low parapet wall at the edge of a pitched or flat roof.

Another form of secret gutter is that formed in a valley – the junction between two adjacent roof slopes – partially hidden by the roof covering materials, such as slates or tiles.

SECRET NAILING A method of nailing wood so that the nail heads cannot be seen. TONGUED-AND-GROOVED boards can be secret-nailed by driving panel pins through the junction between the tongue and shoulder at an angle. When the next board is fixed in place the nail heads are concealed.

Another method is to lift a sliver of wood with a chisel, nail the wood in place, and stick the sliver down.

SECRET SCREWING Also known as pocket screwing. Recesses are cut in woodwork, often at an angle, in order to provide a firm but unobtrusive fixing surface for screws. Secret screwing can be used to fix a table top to its legs or side supports, from underneath.

SECTIONAL TOWER ◗ SCAFFOLDING TOWER

SELF-GRIP WRENCH ◗ WRENCHES

SELF-PRIMING CYLINDER ◗ HOT WATER CYLINDER

SELF-TAPPING SCREWS ◗ SCREWS

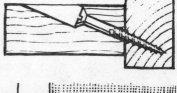

secret screwing

SEMI-PLAIN Wallpaper or vinyl wallcoverings that do not have a matching or repeating motif and can therefore be hung without having to line through with adjacent sheets.

Also known as 'free match'.

(◗ DROP PATTERN; SET PATTERN)

SEPTIC TANK A self-purifying chamber, used for the collection and disposal of sewage in areas – often rural – where there is no main drainage service available. The effluent is collected in an air-tight compartment, broken down by bacterial action and then filters down to an outlet, to drain away in the soil.

(◗ CESSPOOL)

SERRATED-EDGE TROWEL ◗ TROWELS

SERVICE PIPE ⧫ RISING MAIN

SET PATTERN A decorative design or motif on wallpapers or vinyl wall-coverings that is repeated horizontally, across the width of the material, when correctly hung. (⧫ DROP PATTERN; SEMI-PLAIN)

SETTING COAT The final coat of plaster on RENDERING that is about 3 mm (⅛ in.) thick. Also known as the skim coat.

SHAKES Splits in timber often due to stresses set up during seasoning or felling.

SHAVEHOOKS Three different shapes of tool are available, with sharpened steel blades for scraping softened paint from timber mouldings, such as SKIRTINGS and ARCHITRAVES. The three types of shavehook are triangular, pear-shaped, and combination – a straight, a curved, and a concave blade.

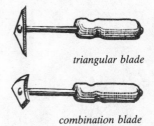

triangular blade

combination blade

Sizes are 175 mm (7 ins.) long.

SHAVER SOCKET The only kind of SOCKET OUTLET permitted by the Institute of Electrical Engineers Regulations (IEE Regs) in a bathroom. The socket is designed to take the plugs on electric shavers only.

SHELLAC A natural orange-colour resin, formed by insects on the bark of trees in India and Thailand, and used as the basis of polish, VARNISH and KNOTTING.

SHELVING STUDS The many methods suitable and the types of fittings manufactured for supporting shelves are numerous, ranging from home-made wooden dowels and metal angle-strips to proprietary fittings.

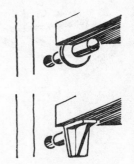

Two of these fittings are the plastic dowel plug, or stud, and the plastic bracket stud. Both are push-fits into pre-drilled holes and both are capable of carrying heavy shelving. Allow at least four studs to a shelf.

SHERARDIZED METAL Iron or steel – coated with a layer of zinc to prevent it corroding. It is a more sophisticated and

141

expensive method than that used for GALVANIZED METAL, but a more accurate and precise process, that helps to preserve the contours of the fitting.

SHINGLES Split or sawn tiles, made of oak or cedar wood, used chiefly as a roof covering – sometimes as a wall cladding.

Shingles are about one-tenth the weight of conventional clay tiles but need to be specially fire-proofed and laid at a steep pitch.

Shingles are wedge-shaped – about 400 mm by 125 mm (16 ins. by 5 ins.) wide, tapering to 6 mm ($\frac{1}{4}$ in.) – and fixed to BATTENS with galvanized nails.

SHIP-LAP CLADDING Horizontal boards, about 150 mm by 25 mm (6 ins. by 1 in.) wide, nailed to vertical BATTENS – the REBATED edge of each board interlocks with the one above it to form a unified and weatherproof cladding material.

(◗ WALL CLADDINGS)

SHOE The shaped portion that fits on to the bottom of a downpipe to direct water into a gully.

(◗ GUTTERS AND DOWNPIPES)

SHOOTING Trueing the edge of a board with a plane.

SHOOTING BOARD A wooden jig made to steady a board while the edges are being planed, particularly END GRAIN timber.

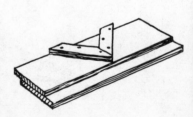

A mitre-shooting board is jigged to facilitate planing the mitred-edges of boards or BATTENS.

SHORING Temporarily supporting part of a structure while making alterations to it.

SHOULDER PLANE ◗ PLANES

SHUTTERING Temporary wooden formwork, used to make a mould for concrete.

SICILIAN TILING ◗ SPANISH TILING

SIGHT SIZE A glazier's term, describing the visible area of glass when a pane has been puttied into its frame. Since it is the actual area that admits daylight, it is also known as the 'daylight size'.

SILENCER A length of plastic tubing screwed into the underside of a BALL VALVE to allow the incoming water supply to discharge into the CISTERN below the existing water level.

Not all local authorities permit the use of a silencer due to the possibility of back-siphonage into the mains supply.

SILICON CARBIDE ◗ ABRASIVES

SILL The bottom horizontal part of a door or window frame, which projects in order to protect the wall beneath it from excessive weathering.

SINGLE-STACK PLUMBING A plumbing system that uses one large pipe, usually 75 mm or 100 mm (3 ins. or 4 ins.) in diameter, into which are fed all the SOIL and WASTE water PIPES in a house.

Occasional exceptions are a kitchen waste pipe from a sink or an appliance on the opposite side of a house – either of which may have its own separate branch connection to the drains.

SIPHONIC CLOSET A relatively silent low-level water closet, in which the contents of the pan are sucked out by siphonage before flushing occurs and the water is replaced.

SIZE Thin glue or paste used to seal the surface of a plastered wall before it is papered. Size seals the surface and prevents the wall absorbing too much of the moisture in the paste.

SKEW NAILING Nails that are driven in at an angle, acute to the surface of the wood, rather than at right angles to it.

Skew nailing is used where two pieces of wood meet at right angles, and no other form of nailing can be used. Alternate nails are often driven in at alternate angles in

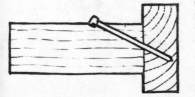

order to create additional strength – a method known as dovetail nailing.

Also known as tosh nailing.

SKIM COAT ♦ SETTING COAT

SKIRTING BOARD A softwood board, nailed to GROUNDS at the bottom of walls, to protect the plaster.

In addition to wooden skirtings, which may be square-edged or moulded, they may also be made of clay, cork or vinyl tiles to match the floor covering and form a continuous surface.

SKYLIGHT ♦ ROOFLIGHT

SLATE Metamorphic stone with a characteristic strata that makes it an easy material to split into thin sheets; it is ideal, therefore, as a roof or WALL-CLADDING material.

Slates are nailed to BATTENS in one of two ways – either through the top edge of each slate (head-nailing) or through the centre (centre-nailing) according to the slope of the roof, the size of the slate and the exposure of the site. Each slate is fixed so that it will overlap a slate in the course next but one below it.

There are three thicknesses of slate, the thickest being 13 mm ($\frac{1}{2}$ in.). Sizes vary from 200 mm to 610 mm (8 ins. to 24 ins.) long and 150 mm to 400 mm (6 ins. to 16 ins.) wide.

SLATE HANGING Slates fixed to horizontal BATTENS on an outside wall – primarily as additional weatherproofing but also for an aesthetic finish.

SLEEPER WALL A dwarf wall, used in SUSPENDED FLOOR construction. The sleeper wall is built on a concrete slab, in honeycomb bond, to facilitate sufficient cross ventilation in the space between the slab and the suspended floor.

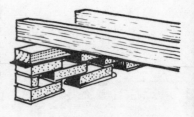

SLEDGE HAMMER ♦ HAMMERS

SLIP-JOINT PLIERS ♦ PLIERS

SLIPSTONES Small, hand-held forms of oilstone used for sharpening special cutting tools.

SLURRY Cement, or sand and cement, mixed with water to the consistency of thin cream. Slurry is often used for temporarily protecting stone or marble during building work, or as a method of filling the joints between ceramic or quarry floor tiles.

SNAPPED FLINT ♦ KNAPPED FLINT

SNAP HEADER A half brick.

SOAKERS Small folded pieces of metal – lead, copper or zinc – or bituminized felt, which are interleaved between alternate tiles or slates to weatherproof the junctions between sloping roofs and adjoining walls, such as chimneys or DORMER windows.

SOCKET OUTLETS Electric supply points for plugs. Modern circuits have 13 amp SOCKET OUTLETS to receive flat, three-pin plugs; older RADIAL-wired systems, may have 2, 5 or 15 amp outlets to receive round-pin (two or three pins) plugs, of different sizes.

SOCKET WRENCH ♦ SPANNERS

SOFFIT The underside of an arch. Also the horizontal boarding fixed to the feet of projecting RAFTERS at EAVES' level.

SOFTWOOD The wood from coniferous trees that is used for the majority of structural work, as well as painted joinery, such as built-in furniture, SKIRTING BOARDS, DOOR LININGS and ARCHITRAVES.

Softwood may be bought sawn or planed: sawn timber is roughly finished; planed timber is smooth.

The sizes of planed softwood are slightly less than the sawn (or NOMINAL) size. For example, a piece of 100 mm by 50 mm (4 ins. by 2 ins.) softwood will, when planed all round (PAR), be about 98 mm by 48 mm ($3\frac{7}{8}$ ins. by $1\frac{7}{8}$ ins.).

SOIL OR STACK PIPE A vertical pipe, usually 75 mm or 100 mm (3 ins. or 4 ins.) in diameter, in house plumbing systems that conveys effluence from the house to the DRAINS.

SOLDIER ARCH A flat arch, consisting of uncut bricks, laid on end, i.e. on their HEADER faces. The arch is supported either by an angle iron on the bottom inner edge of the wall, and bearing on each side of it, or by various other means, such as metal cramps.

SOLE PLATE The bottom horizontal timber used at floor level when building a STUD PARTITION. The sole plate may be screwed or nailed to the floorboards and joists or, on a solid floor, fixed by ANCHOR BOLTS to the concrete. The sole plate not only provides fixings for the uprights in a partition but also helps to spread the weight of the framework over the floor surface.

SOLID PUNCH Used to punch small holes – up to a maximum of 6 mm ($\frac{1}{4}$ in.) in diameter – in thin sheet metal.

SPACE HEATING ◗ CENTRAL HEATING

SPALLING Surface flaking of bricks or stones as they weather – particularly in exposed situations where moisture in the material freezes, expands, and causes the surface of the brick or stone to break off.

SPAN The distance between two points of support; for example, the span of an arch is the distance between the parts of the wall that support it.

SPANDREL The area of wall beneath the bottom of a window and the top of the one directly beneath it. Also describes the triangular space beneath a staircase.

SPANISH TILING A combination of two types of clay roofing tiles – 'overs' and 'unders' – that interlock. Both types are half-round and tapered, but the under tiles are slightly wider and shallower in section.

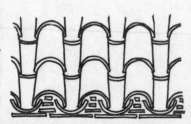

Also known as Sicilian tiling.

(♦ ITALIAN TILING)

SPANNERS The right size spanner is essential – the wrong size will damage the corners of a nut or bolt and be likely to slip, causing grazed knuckles.

There is a multiplicity of thread systems in use, but in most cases non-adjustable spanners have the sizes of the nuts and bolts they are made to fit, stamped or impressed into them.

There is also a wide variety of spanner-types. Those in common use fall within the following groups:

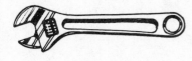

Adjustable (Crescent wrench) As the name implies the spanner has jaws that can be adjusted to fit any size of nut or bolt. However, the adjustable is weaker than a purpose-made spanner, and is also liable to slip if over-strained for the jaws will, in time, work loose.

As a general-purpose spanner (when the correct size is not available) it is an invaluable substitute.

Box A hollow tubular spanner, designed to fit over the top of a recessed hexagonal nut – such as an IN SITU sparking plug. Box spanners have a fixed tommy bar (or holes in the shank through which a bar can be passed) in order to give the user extra leverage.

Combination A spanner that is open at one end and has a ring at the other – a useful general purpose tool.

Open ended Most spanners are open ended, i.e. they can be fitted round a nut from the side. But their main advantage is that they can be used where access is limited, since the jaws are at an angle of 15° to the shaft of the spanner. By moving the spanner through 30°, turning it over and repeating the process, it is possible to tighten or remove a nut within this limited angle of space.

Ring These are closed spanners that fit

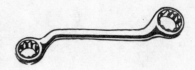

snugly over a nut or bolt to provide a firmer grip and greater leverage than an open-ended spanner. The inside of the ring may have six or twelve sides (known as a six-point, or twelve-point spanner, respectively) to engage the corners of a hexagonal or square-headed nut or bolt.

Ring spanners may have the head in the same plane as the shaft or be offset in order to give increased accessibility – known, respectively, as plain and offset spanners.

Socket This is the most sophisticated of all types of spanner, with a range of interchangeable heads (or sockets) that can be fitted to a speed brace (or cranked handle), or a variety of bar handles, including a ratchet driver.

(♦ ALLEN KEY; WRENCHES)

SPAR Alternative term for RAFTER.

SPAR DASH ♦ ROUGHCAST

SPATTERDASH A mixture of sand and cement thrown on to a relatively smooth wall – say flush-faced brickwork or stone – in order to provide a 'key' for a coat of plaster.

(♦ TYROLEAN FINISH)

SPECIAL GRANTS ♦ GRANTS

SPECIFICATION A written document – often prepared by an architect or surveyor – which describes the materials to be used and the standards of workmanship expected in executing a contract. A specification is normally supported by a set of detailed WORKING DRAWINGS.

(♦ CONTRACT)

SPIRAL RATCHET SCREW-DRIVER ♦ SCREWDRIVERS

SPIRIT LEVEL A metal, hardwood or plastic-framed tool, containing one or more glass or plastic tubes. Each tube is slightly bow-shaped and contains either alcohol, chloroform or oil, and a small bubble of air.

When the tool is held so that the tube is horizontal the bubble rises to the highest point and settles between two marked lines to register 'level'.

The simplest form of spirit level has a single tube but many incorporate three – one set in line with the length of the tool, and two more at right angles to it, the latter facilitating the user to check verticals as well as horizontals.

Sizes vary from small pocket-size levels 75 mm (3 ins.) long to 1000 mm (roughly 1 yd).

SPIRIT STAIN A wood stain, made from dye dissolved in methylated spirits, that dries rapidly and does not conceal the grain of the wood.

SPLIT-RING CONNECTOR ◗ TIM-BER CONNECTOR

SPOKESHAVE ◗ PLANES

SPOT BOARD A piece of board, about 750 mm (30 ins.) square, on which plaster is knocked up, i.e. reworking a mixture into a plastic state after it has partly set. Marine plywood is the ideal material but blockboard or hardboard can be used.

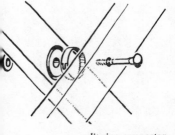

split-ring connector

SPRAY TAP ◗ taps

SPRIG ◗ NAILS

SPRINGING LINE The level, estab-lished as an imaginary horizontal line, from which an arch 'springs' or rises to span an opening.

SPUR An extra length of cable supplying power to additional SOCKET OUTLETS, off the route of the ring circuit – either a maximum of two 13 amp sockets, or an appliance rated at a maximum of 3000 WATTS.

SQUARE JOINT ◗ BUTT JOINT

SQUARED RUBBLE Stone walling that is built with roughly squared stones of different sizes. A squared rubble wall may have the stones lining through horizontally (i.e. coursed) every third or fourth stone. (◗ RUBBLE WALLING)

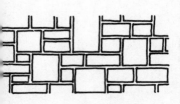

SQUARES The combination square is a precision-made metal tool, that can be used to set out 45° (for mitred joints) and 90° angles. Also used as a depth gauge. The blade is engraved as a rule, and can be removed from the tool and used for measuring work or as a straight edge. See right.

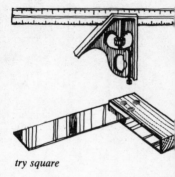

try square

The try square has a steel blade and a hardwood stock and is the woodworker's essential tool for setting out or checking right angles.

The blade lengths vary from 150 mm to 300 mm (6 ins. to 12 ins.).

SQUARE SAWN Timber that has been cut to a rectangular cross section.

SQUINT QUOIN ▶ QUOIN

STABLE DOOR A door that is made and hung in two parts, so that the top half can be opened while the bottom remains closed. Useful as a means of confining small children or animals, such as in a rear kitchen.

STACK A brick chimney, containing one or more flues grouped together and passing through a roof.

STAGGERED JOINTS The jointing method used when fixing panels of sheet material to a framework in order to achieve the same effect as bonding, thereby minimizing possible lines of weakness. For example, when fixing sheets of PLASTERBOARD to a STUD PARTITION, hairline cracks between adjacent boards are less likely to occur if they are laid with staggered (or broken) joints.

STAIRCASE ▶ CARRIAGE PIECE; DOG-LEG STAIR; KITE WINDER; NEWEL CAP; NEWEL POST; OPEN RISER; OPEN WELL; RISER; TREADS; STRINGS

STAPLES ▶ NAILS

STAVE A ladder rung.

STAY BAR A horizontal metal bar that reinforces a LEADED-LIGHT, or a MULLIONED window.

STEEL FLOAT ▶ FLOATS

STEEL RULE ▶ RULES

STEEL TAPE ◗ RULES

STEPPED FLASHING A metal or fibre FLASHING that is tailored to weatherproof the junction between a sloping roof and an adjoining wall – for example, the junction between a chimney stack passing through a roof. The flashing is cut in a series of steps and tucked into brick COURSES, so that there is a weatherproof skirting, at least 150 mm (6 ins.) high.

STILE One of the outer uprights, forming part of a framed door or window, into which horizontal rails are tenoned, i.e. jointed.

STILSON ◗ WRENCHES

STIPPLING BRUSH ◗ PAINT BRUSHES

STIRRUP ◗ JOIST HANGER

STOCKS ◗ BRICKS

STONE FLAGS ◗ STONE SLATES

STONE SLATES Thin slabs of sandstone used as roofing material in rural areas. Thick, heavy slabs are referred to as stone flags – used chiefly in the Pennines; the thinner and lighter slabs are used primarily in the Cotswolds and Wales.

Stone slates are fixed to roof timbers with oak pegs.

STONEWARE Ceramic material that is used for some drainage components. Clay containing flint and sand is fired and given a salt-glazed finish to make strong, non-porous fittings.

STOPCOCK A tap in a pipe that can be opened or closed to control the supply of water flowing through it. There are usually two stopcocks to a house: one is outside and below ground, covered by a cast-iron plate and reached by a long-handled key made of wood; the second stopcock is inside the house. This is usually at the point where the service pipe or RISING MAIN ascends to feed the cold water supply tank.

The internal stopcock controls the internal supply; the outside stopcock controls the supply to the house.

Also known as a stop valve.

(♦ TAPS)

STOPPED CHAMFER ♦ CHAMFER

STOPPED END The end of a wall bonded to finish flush.

STOPPED HOUSING ♦ HOUSED JOINT

STOPPING A paste used to fill small holes in woodwork prior to rubbing it down and painting it. There are two types of stopping material – hard, for interior use, and waterproof, for exterior work.

Proprietary stopping can be bought in a range of colours to match different coloured woods – useful when wood is to be finished but left unpainted for polishing or staining.

Hard stopping can also be made with two parts of putty, one of white lead and little gold size.

STOP VALVE ♦ STOPCOCK

STORAGE HEATER ♦ CENTRAL HEATING

STOREY ROD A long straight strip of timber used by bricklayers when setting out brickwork or steps. The rod – sometimes known as a gauge rod – has brick COURSES or step heights marked on it and is used as a check when building, to ensure the work rises at the correct height.

Storey rods were originally the full height of a storey but nowadays they are usually about 2 m (6 ft 6 ins.).

A rod is useful to the handyman when building new metric brickwork to tie in with existing imperial brickwork.

S-TRAP ♦ TRAPS

STRETCHER A brick laid with its width at right angles to the wall, so that one of its long faces is exposed.

(♦ BONDS; BRICKS; HEADER)

STRETCHER BOND ♦ BONDS

STRIKER PLATE ♦ KEEPER PLATE

STRING COURSE A row of bricks or stones that project slightly from the face of an outer wall to provide a horizontal band as a feature.

STRINGS The timber boards on the sides of some staircases into which the TREADS and RISERS are housed. A closed string has parallel sides; a cut string has the board cut to the profile of the steps; and a wall string is one fixed against a wall.

STRIPPING KNIFE A knife for stripping wallpaper or softened paint off walls. The blade is similar to a FILLING KNIFE but is available in broader widths – up to 125 mm (5 ins.) across – and is more rigid.

STRUCTURAL WALL Any wall that supports another part of the structure in addition to its own weight. A load-bearing wall.

STRUTTING Pieces of timber used in a roof truss or frame as stiffeners – each piece, or strut, is able to resist compressive strains.

On some floors of a wide SPAN herringbone strutting is used to stiffen and strengthen them. BATTENS, or similar strips of SOFTWOOD are arranged in pairs and fixed diagonally, between the floor joists.

STUBBY SCREWDRIVER ♦ SCREW-DRIVERS

STUB TENON ♦ TENON

STUCCO A smooth-finished surfacing – usually CEMENT, LIME and SAND – applied to the outer face of a wall.

STUD PARTITION A timber-framed wall that provides a base framework for a covering of plasterboard, lath and plaster, or match-boarding.

A stud partition may be constructed to be LOAD-BEARING, i.e. carrying part of the floor or structure above it, by the addition of diagonal struts. This is known as a trussed partition.

SUB-FRAME A wooden frame that is fitted into a window opening to provide a fixing surface for a metal window. A sub-frame can more easily be weatherproofed to an opening than a metal window.

SUFFOLK LATCH ♦ NORFOLK LATCH

SUGAR SOAP A caustic-based material used for washing down paintwork.

SUPAGLYPTA ♦ WALL COVERINGS

SUPATAP ♦ TAPS

SURFORM ♦ RASPS

SUSPENDED CEILING A false ceiling, i.e. one that is suspended from the floor or roof above, with the space between the two used to conceal wiring, pipework or ventilation trunking. A suspended ceiling may also be used solely for aesthetic reasons.

SUSPENDED FLOOR A timber floor that is supported at each end by structural walls. Suspended floors may be on an upper storey, or on a ground level floor that is supported by JOISTS resting on honeycomb brick sleeper walls.

SWAN NECK A purpose-made pipe, used in some rainwater systems, that provides a gently curved connection between the gutter on overhanging EAVES and a DOWNPIPE fixed to the wall beneath.

SWEPT VALLEY A junction between two sloping roofs that is joined with special tiles or slates, cut to a tapered shape. The junction sweeps round in a gentle curve, unlike the sharp intersection formed on its 'sister' construction – the LACED VALLEY.
(♦ VALLEY GUTTER)

SWG The abbreviation used for standard wire gauge – the term describing the thickness of steel wire, stainless steel and non-ferrous metals. For example, 20 swg equals 0.036 in. Swg designations are, however, in the process of being phased out in favour of metric sizes.

SWITCHES Devices that make and break an electric circuit by means of metal contacts that open and close when a lever or button is operated.

A two-way switch allows a light to be switched on or off from two places; a multiple switch from two or more places.

A pull-cord switch controls a light, fan or radiant-heater by means of a cord. It is used where a conventional switch would be dangerous if used by someone with wet hands, for instance near a kitchen sink or in a bathroom.

A dimmer switch can vary the level of illumination from a dull glow to the maximum brightness of a lamp's WATTAGE. It can be fitted as a replacement for a conventional light switch.

(◆ TIME SWITCH)

SYNTHETIC RESINS Artificially produced resins, such as urea and melamine, that are used in the manufacture of certain adhesives. Synthetic resins are rot-proof and moisture-proof, and therefore particularly suited to the manufacture of laminated boards, such as blockboard and plywood, and plastics.

T

TACK RAG Cheesecloth impregnated with slow-drying varnish for wiping off the last specks of dust from a surface, after RUBBING DOWN and before painting.

Tack rag can also be bought as a sheet of impregnated gauze, which is folded several times to provide a pad shape.

TANALIZED TIMBER Wood that has been industrially impregnated with a preservative.

TANK CUTTER ◆ BITS

TANKING A method of damp-proofing the floor and walls of a basement, or part of a wall that is below ground level. The walls are built with an inner and outer skin. The inner skin, which may be brick or concrete, is the structural one, coated on the outside with a damp-proof material – such as 19 mm (¾ in.) asphalt. The outer skin – a half-brick thick wall – sandwiches the asphalt between both walls and protects it from being punctured by the BACKFILL material.

The asphalt between the walls is linked to the horizontal DPC in the floor, to form a continuous waterproof barrier.
(◆ DAMP-PROOF COURSE)

TAPS Valves for controlling the flow of water – providing draw-off points for supplies coming from a COLD WATER CISTERN or HOT WATER CYLINDER.

There are many different types but most fall within the following categories:
Bib This has an horizontal inlet supply pipe and is generally found on the outside wall of a house as a tap to provide water for garden purposes or car-washing. It sometimes has a screw-thread end for connecting to hose pipes.

156

Mixer A tap that has two pillar taps united by a common outlet, so that hot and cold water is mixed as it is drawn off.

Non-concussive A tap controlled by a lever rather than the conventional screwdown valve in order to avoid the vibration that can be caused by WATER HAMMER.

Pillar A tap with a vertical fixing and a supply pipe coming in underneath. Pillar taps are used on most baths, wash basins and sinks.

Spray A tap that mixes hot and cold water and delivers a spray, the supply and temperature of the water controlled by a knob.

Supatap A tap with a revolving nozzle. It prevents WATER HAMMER and has the added advantage that the supply need not be turned off when changing the washer.

 **TEMPLET (Template)** A metal, wood or card pattern, used to simulate the profile of a moulded shape for setting-out purposes.

Proprietary shape-tracing tools are available.

TENON The reduced or narrowed end of a piece of wood that is cut to fit a mating hole – or mortise – in a second piece of wood to make a MORTISE-AND-TENON JOINT.

A stub tenon is one that does not go right through the wood in which the mortise is cut.

TENON SAW ⬧ SAWS

TERRACOTTA Hard burnt and once-fired clay, nowadays used chiefly as a lightweight CLADDING or for moulded ornamental work. Terracotta varies from yellow ochre to reddish-brown and has a smooth finish, which is generally left unglazed.

TERRAZZO Marble chippings of various colours, laid in a matrix of white or coloured cement.

Terrazzo is used to give a surface finish – about 19 mm (¾ in.) thick – to a sound base, e.g. a sand and cement SCREED.

When dry, the terrazzo is ground to a smooth surface that emphasizes the natural colours of the stones. It can also be given a non-slip finish.

Also known as Venetian mosaic.

TESSERA The small cubes or polygonal shapes of marble, stone, glass or pottery, used to make MOSAIC.

THATCH A traditional roofing material, used chiefly in rural areas, made from straw or reed.

Roofs thatched with straw can last up to twenty years, those thatched with reed from thirty to sixty years, according to the type of reed used. Thatch is secured to battens on RAFTERS, with metal pins and hazel sticks or willow saplings.

THERMAL INSULATION ♦ INSULATING MATERIALS

THERMAL MOVEMENT The movement that occurs when materials expand and contract due to temperature changes. Many fittings are designed to accommodate this movement by including EXPANSION JOINTS.

THERMOSTAT A device that opens and closes an electric circuit when a preselected temperature is reached. Thermostats may be used in conjunction with central heating systems, individual radiator controls, and IMMERSION HEATERS to control water temperature.

T-HINGE ♦ HINGES

THINNERS ♦ PAINT

THIXOTROPIC PAINT ♦ PAINTS

THREE-PLY ♦ PLYWOOD

THROAT A narrow groove cut in the underside of a projecting window sill or threshold to prevent rainwater creeping back under it through capillary action. The throat helps rainwater to drip clear of the wall below, hence it is also known as a drip groove.

A throat also describes the gap at the base of a fireplace flue – just above the opening – often fitted with a damper to control the drawing power of the fire.

THUMB LATCH ♦ NORFOLK LATCH

TIE BEAM A beam that prevents the feet of opposing rafters from spreading. Tie beams may be timber, steel rods, or a combination of both.

TILE-AND-A-HALF A purpose-made tile, which is half as wide again as a plain TILE, used in roofing to ensure the tiling finishes flush at the EAVES. A tile-and-a-half is also used at the edges of a VALLEY GUTTER.

TILE CUTTER A pointed tungsten-tipped steel tool, used to scribe the glazed surface of ceramic tiles in order to snap them.

TILE HANGING Plain clay roofing tiles used as a WALL CLADDING. The tiles are hung on TILING BATTENS.

TILING BATTENS Strips of softwood, usually 50 mm by 25 mm (2 ins. by 1 in.) or 38 mm by 19 mm (1½ ins. by ¾ in.), which are nailed at right angles to roof rafters to provide fixings for SLATES, TILES or SHINGLES.

A counter-battened roof has tiling battens nailed through a layer of untearable felt to the rafters, and in line with them; a second layer of battens is then fixed at right angles to the first. This is more expensive construction than conventional battening, but it allows moisture that gets below the roof covering to drain to the gutters. It also helps a roof to breathe.

TILTING FILLET A length of softwood, triangular in cross-section, that may be used at the foot of RAFTERS on a sloping roof, to tilt the bottom row of tiles. This row, which is two tiles thick, is therefore able to fit more snugly together.

TIMBER CONNECTOR Patent metal fixing, used to increase the shear strength of joints between adjacent timbers in a framework or roof truss.

Connectors may be toothed or corrugated rings, or split rings that are recessed into specially cut grooves.

TIME SWITCH A switch that is operated by an electric or mechanical clock. At its simplest, a time switch will turn an appliance on or off at a pre-set time; more sophisticated types are capable of more complex controls, spanning a 24 hour period.

Time switches may be integral parts of an appliance, e.g. in an electric cooker or central heating boiler; or they may be portable fittings that can be plugged into SOCKET OUTLETS to control a light, heater or electric blanket.

TOGGLE BOLT ♦ WALL FIXINGS

TONGUED-AND-GROOVED BOARDING Softwood boards which are jointed edge to edge to provide a flat flush surface. Each board has a groove cut in one edge and a tongue (to correspond with the groove) in the other. Also called match boarding.

Tongued, grooved and V-jointed boarding has one face of the tongued-edged chamfered, so that when adjacent boards fit together they present a V-shaped groove.

Tongue-and-grooved boarding is used for good quality flooring – being both dust- and draught-proof.

Tongued-and-grooved and V-jointed boarding is often used for ceilings or WALL CLADDING.

TOOTHING If a brick wall is to be extended at a later date, the end of the wall is left with alternate COURSES of brickwork projecting, so that when the wall is finished the BOND will be maintained.

If a brick wall is to have another built at right angles to it at a later date, the first wall has indentations left in alternate courses to facilitate a soundly bonded junction between them.

TORCHING Sand and cement mortar used to seal the joints between slates or tiles to exclude wind or rain.

Torching is used less nowadays since CAPILLARY ACTION can cause moisture to creep between the mortar and the covering and rot the TILING BATTENS.

TORQUE WRENCH ♦ WRENCHES

TOSH NAILING ♦ SKEW NAILING

TOUCH DRY Paint or adhesive that is dry enough to be touched without sticking to the fingertips or leaving fingermarks.

Surfaces coated with certain contact ADHESIVES need to be touch dry before they are pressed together.

TRANSLUCENT GLASS ♦ GLASS

TRANSOM The horizontal part of a door frame that separates the door from a fanlight above it. Also one or more horizontal bars – made of stone, metal or wood – that separate the fixed and opening portions of a window.

TRAPS Every bath, basin, sink, bidet or water closet has a U-shaped bend in the outlet pipe underneath, containing water.

This water seal – or trap – prevents odours returning from the main sewers and is automatically replenished every time the appliance is flushed.

There are two kinds: the P-trap, which has a horizontal outlet, and the S-trap with a vertical outlet – providing alternative connections to the WASTE PIPES.

The lowest point of a trap has a screw-plug in the underside so that a blockage can easily be cleared.

In addition to P- and S-traps which describe the shape of a pipe connection, there are also bottle traps. These are proprietary fittings that achieve the same effect, plumbed in between an appliance and its waste pipe. The bottom half of a bottle trap can be unscrewed to clear a blockage.

TREADS The flat or horizontal surfaces of a step.

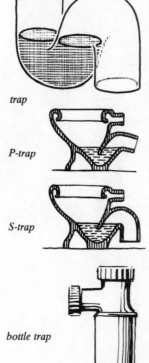

trap

P-trap

S-trap

bottle trap

TRIMMING KNIFE A general-purpose knife used for such jobs as trimming cork or plastic floor coverings, laminates or card. Also known as a Stanley knife, it has interchangeable blades that are kept inside the hollow metal handle.

TROWELS ◆ ANGLE TROWEL; BRICKLAYER'S TROWEL; FLOATS

TRUSSED PARTITION ◆ STUD PARTITION

TRY SQUARE ◆ SQUARES

TURPENTINE SUBSTITUTE An oil-paint thinner made from a distillation of petroleum, that is a cheaper alternative to turpentine.

TWIST BITS ◆ BITS

TWO-BOLT LOCK ◆ LOCKS AND LATCHES

TWO-COAT WORK ◆ PAINTS

TWO-PART PAINTS ◆ PAINTS

TWO-WAY SWITCH ◆ SWITCHES

TYROLEAN FINISH A cement and sand finish applied to external brick walls to improve their weathering qualities and appearance. Tyrolean RENDERING, applied with a manually-controlled machine, gives a rough-textured finish that can be decorated with masonry paint.

U

UNDERCOAT ♦ PAINT
UNDERFLOOR HEATING ♦ CENTRAL HEATING
UNDERPINNING A method of strengthening an existing foundation with concrete which may or may not be reinforced.
UNDERTILES ♦ ITALIAN TILING
UNIVERSAL BEAM A steel beam that is similar to but stronger than the now largely superseded ROLLED STEEL JOIST, and used for both columns and BEAMS.
UNWROT Also known as unwrought or 'undressed' timber – i.e. timber which is sawn but not planed. Unwrot is often used on WORKING DRAWINGS and SPECIFICATIONS.
UPSTAND The part of a metal-covered roof that is turned up against an adjacent wall. The upright portion is generally weathered by a separate cover FLASHING.

Upstand also describes a beam that projects upwards, above a floor level – commonly seen above window openings.
U-VALUE The unit of thermal transmittance, i.e. the number of BTUs that will pass through 1 sq ft of material, in one hour, for every 1°F difference between the two sides of the material. In metric terms this is expressed in WATTS per sq. m per °C difference in temperature.

The better the insulating qualities of a material the lower its U-value. Many materials have a U-value assigned to them by manufacturers, which can be used when calculating the U-value of a wall or roof, when there may be several materials forming a sandwich construction.
(♦ BRITISH THERMAL UNIT)

V

VALLEY GUTTER A rainwater gutter formed IN SITU between the adjacent slopes of a pitched roof. The gutter has a softwood board providing a base surface between the rafters and is lined with lead, zinc or bituminous felt.

(◊ LACED VALLEY; SWEPT VALLEY)

VALVES Devices that turn on or off the flow of water, oil or gas in a pipe. For example, a STOPCOCK or STOP VALVE on a mains supply pipe, or a BALL VALVE.

VANITY UNIT A unit consisting of a MELAMINE laminated surface, with a ceramic or stainless steel wash-basin set within it. The front of the unit is usually preformed with a rounded edge and the back swept up to form a small raised ledge; the joint between the basin and the plastic is covered with a waterproof seal.

Suitable for bedroom or bathroom, a vanity unit is ideal for use in a built-in cupboard where space is limited.

VAPOUR BARRIER A design feature, sometimes used in building construction, that prevents warm, moist air passing from one part of a building into a cold wall or ceiling and causing hidden condensation. For example, an impervious layer of material, such as ALUMINIUM FOIL or bitumen impregnated paper, fixed to CEILING JOISTS (above the plasterboard) will prevent water vapour condensing in the roof space above.

VARNISH A spirit or oil-based solution that can be applied, like paint, to give unpainted or stained wood a transparent and protective film. Varnish may have a

164

3333333443334333333333

glossy, sheen or matt finish.

Spirit-based varnishes, such as resin dissolved in alcohol, dry rapidly.

(♦ POLYURETHANE VARNISH)

VENEER A thin layer of hardwood used to give a decorative finish to less attractive wood, such as that used for some furniture, or for facing manufactured boards, such as blockboard or plywood. According to how it is cut, the veneer may be arranged in various ways to create different aesthetic effects.

VENEER HAMMER ♦ HAMMERS

VENTILATING BRICK ♦ AIR BRICK

VENETIAN MOSAIC ♦ TERRAZZO

VENETIAN WINDOW A three-part window, with the tallest part in the middle with a round arch, flanked by flat arched openings.

VENTILATING PIPE A pipe, open at the top, that ventilates a SOIL or WASTE PIPE. Often the soil pipe serving the highest water closet in a house is continued up above roof level to act as a ventilating pipe.

Also referred to as a vent stack.

(♦ SOIL PIPE)

VENT STACK ♦ VENTILATING PIPE

VERDIGRIS The protective film – usually green or greenish-blue – that ultimately appears on the surface of copper or bronze after it has been exposed to the atmosphere; the result of oxidization.

VERGE Tiles or slates that project over the edge of a roof to protect the wall beneath it.

VERMICULITE ♦ INSULATING MATERIALS

VERTICAL BOARDING ♦ TONGUED-AND-GROOVED BOARDING

VICE A metal device that can be fixed to a work bench or table to hold a workpiece – such as a piece of timber – firm while sawing, drilling etc.

A woodworker's vice has a steel body and mechanism with two cast iron jaws: one fixed and one movable. The jaw widths and their opening capacities vary from 150 mm to 262 mm (6 ins. to 10 ins.) and 112 mm to 375 mm (4½ ins. to 14¾ ins.) respectively.

An engineer's vice has a cast-iron and steel body and is designed to withstand heavier use, such as metal-working.

A portable vice, having aluminium jaws and designed to be clamped to a table top, can be used for lightweight jobs.
(♦ HOLDFAST)

VINYL PAINT ♦ PAINT

VINYL WALLCOVERING ♦ WALLCOVERINGS

V-JOINT ♦ TONGUED-AND-GROOVED BOARDING

VOLT The unit measurement of electric pressure – or force – that causes current to flow in a circuit.

VYNAGLYPTA ♦ WALL COVERINGS

engineer's vice

portable vice

WAGTAIL ◆ PARTING SLIP

WAINSCOT Wood panelling on a wall up to DADO height. So named because wainscot oak – imported from central and eastern Europe – was originally used for this kind of panelling.

WALLBOARD ◆ WALL CLADDING

WALL BRUSH ◆ PAINT BRUSHES

WALL CANVAS ◆ WALL COVERINGS

WALL CLADDING The protective or decorative covering applied to the outer walls of a house. This includes vertical or horizontal boarding, SLATE, SHINGLE or TILE HANGING.

Sheet material, such as wood or plastic laminated man-made boards, are sometimes referred to as internal cladding.

WALL COVERINGS A variety of other materials, in addition to traditional wallpapers, are available for giving decorative finishes to interior walls.

Chief among these are:

Anaglypta A stout, heavily-embossed paper made from cotton fibres, which is available in a range of regular and random designs. It provides a practical covering for plaster walls and ceilings that are sound but surface crazed – cracks must be filled first, however, and can be painted with EMULSION.

Supaglypta and Vynaglypta are two higher relief papers than Anaglypta, but used for the same purpose. The heaviest of these is Vynaglypta, consisting of a layer of clear PVC laminated to a stout paper. It is easier to strip off than the other relief papers.

Cork Paper-thin panels of cork, in irregular shapes, laminated to a paper backing. A range of natural colours is available including some with an overprinted pattern. A LINING PAPER must be used first.

Grasscloth Strands of grass and flakes of bark sewn together and glued to a paper backing. Other types are made with similar natural materials, such as flax, hemp and jute.

All are difficult for the amateur to hang successfully and will not withstand hard wear; but they do have the look of luxury about them and can make an effective focus of interest.

Hessian (Wall canvas) Natural or furnishing hessian – which is coarsely woven with a sacklike weave – is the cheapest of all. Finer textured hessian in natural (unprepared) or dyed colours can be bought unbacked, or backed with paper, latex or foam to make it easier to handle and hang.

Hessian can be painted with OIL PAINT or EMULSION.

Lincrusta A traditional, heavily moulded material, manufactured from linseed oil and a variety of fillers bonded to a flat backing paper. A tough, durable covering, it is made in textured designs as well as simulated materials, such as fabrics, stonework, tiles, and wood panelling.

Lincrusta is available in ready decorated and undecorated finishes.

Vinyl The most versatile of all wall coverings – tough, durable, easy to clean and resistant to water and steam. It is made from stout paper or woven cotton, laminated with a clear PVC, to present a surface that can be lightly scrubbed – ideal, therefore, for bathrooms and kitchens.

Vinyl coverings are both easy to handle and hang, and have the added virtue of being easy to strip off again when necessary.

They are available in a large range of

designs and textures, with finishes varying from a high sheen to a matt surface.

(♠ WALL TILING)

WALL FIXINGS Since plaster, brick and concrete are hard materials into which nails and screws cannot easily be driven, there are a number of proprietary fittings available that simplify fixings. There are many different types of fitting manufactured but the following three groups embrace most types:

Wall plugs Small tubes or cylinders of wood, fibre, metal, nylon or plastic that are inserted into pre-drilled holes in solid walls. As each fixing screw is driven home the plug expands and grips the inside of the hole.

Toggles There are two basic types – gravity and spring-loaded – both made for making fixings to hollow surfaces, such as a plasterboard wall or ceiling. Gravity toggles have a swivel piece that drops into the vertical plane, once the end of the bolt has been pushed through a pre-drilled hole in the surface. The spring-loaded toggle has two 'wings' that are depressed while the toggle is being pushed into place but spring open once through the wall.

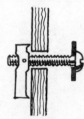

Both can then be tightened to bite into the back of the wall, but neither can be recovered intact once they have been positioned.

(♠ ANCHOR BOLTS)

WALLPAPER One of the traditional materials used as a covering for internally plastered walls.

Finished, i.e. ready-trimmed wallpaper, is usually sold in rolls nominally 10.05 m (approximately 11 yds) long and nominally 530 mm (approximately 21 ins.) wide. Some papers have a margin and need to be trimmed before use – a service offered by most suppliers.

Papers vary in weight, thickness and quality, and may be machine- or hand-printed – the latter being the better quality of the two and often the most expensive. Thin papers are the cheapest but are more liable to tear when wet and stretch if too much paste is applied to them. Thicker, heavier papers are more difficult to handle and hang but are better able to conceal minor defects in a wall's surface.

Other papers are as follows:

Embossed Paper that has a design impressed into it by metal rollers during manufacture. The designs simulate leather, fabrics and wood grain. Duplex embossed papers have a higher relief and are more stretch resistant.

Flock A heavy quality paper that has a surface texture resembling the pile of velvet – the result of gluing fabric fibres to the surface during manufacture.

Lining paper An 'undercoat' paper that is used on all good quality wallpapering jobs. The lining paper – used for walls and ceilings – provides a surface with an even porosity and a good base for the more expensive decorative papers.

Lining papers are available in different grades and, unless painted or papered, turn yellow in a short time. They should always be pasted to a surface so that they are at right angles to the finishing paper.

Ingrain (Woodchip) A paper manufactured by sandwiching minute woodchips and sawdust between two layers of paper. The surface – resembling oatmeal – can be obtained in medium and coarse finishes and, like embossed paper, will help to conceal slight irregularities in the surface of walls and ceilings. Ingrain paper is most effective when decorated with EMULSION paint.

Pre-pasted Paper manufactured with an adhesive-backed surface. The paper is simply cut to length and dipped in a trough of water, when it is ready to hang.

Washable Patterned wallpapers that are

coated during manufacture with a transparent resin emulsion which can be wiped clean with a damp cloth or sponge.

Washable papers are suitable therefore for kitchens, bathrooms and playrooms. The paper cannot, however, be scrubbed like a VINYL wall covering.
(◗ WALL TILING)

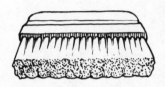

WALLPAPERING BRUSH A wide handled brush – 190 mm to 250 mm (7½ ins. to 10 ins.) – used to smooth freshly pasted wallpaper to a wall. The edge of the bristles is used to tap paper into corners or around projections, such as light switches, fireplaces, etc.

WALL PLATE A length of sawn SOFTWOOD, either 100 mm by 75 mm (4 ins. by 3 ins.) or 75 mm by 50 mm (3 ins. by 2 in.) used horizontally on brick, or building block walls to spread the load and provide a sound base to support flooring or ceiling JOISTS, and RAFTERS.

WALL PLUGS ◗ WALL FIXINGS

WALL STRING ◗ STRING

WALL TIES Strips of plastic, or GALVANIZED METAL or wire, built into a cavity wall during construction, in order to tie the two skins together. The shape of the ties prevents water bridging the gap from the outer skin to the inner.

WALL TILING ◗ CERAMIC TILES; CORK TILES; MOSAICS

WANEY EDGE Bark that is still attached to the edge of SQUARE SAWN timber. Waney edge boarding, such as elm, is often used to clad SPANDRELS.

WARPING The twisting that sometimes occurs in the length of unseasoned wood as it dries out.
(◗ SEASONING)

WARRINGTON HAMMER ◗ HAMMERS

WASHABLE PAPER ◗ WALLPAPERS

WASH-LEATHER GLAZING Glass secured in a door or window by being bedded in a strip of chamois leather and held in position by hardwood strips screwed to the framework. Sometimes used for internal doors or windows, such as in a screen.

WASTE PIPE A pipe that carries waste water from a bath, basin or sink to the drains.

WASTE WATER PREVENTER The CISTERN – which may be high or low level – containing the water that flushes a water closet.

WATER BAR A strip of galvanized iron, about 6 mm ($\frac{1}{4}$ in.) thick, set into a HARDWOOD sill, or a groove in concrete or stone bedded in place with white lead PUTTY or bituminous MASTIC.

A water bar prevents rainwater and draughts being blown between the gap beneath doors and window sills in bad weather.

WATER HAMMER A loud reverberating noise, accompanied by vibration, that may occur in plumbing pipework when a tap is used.

Water hammer may be due to a BALL FLOAT bouncing on the surface of the water as a CISTERN is being refilled, or to uneven stresses set up by water within the pipework – often the result of a poorly designed layout.

The first may be cured by repacking the gland nut on the affected TAP or fitting a SILENCER; the second fault may be cured by fitting an air chamber to the BALL VALVE.

Fitting a non-concussive tap may also cure water hammer.
(◊ TAPS)

WATER REPELLENTS Colourless proprietary fluids that can be applied to external brick- or woodwork to improve their moisture-resistant properties.

WATER SOFTENER An appliance used to soften the domestic water supply in a HARD WATER area. Hard water, which is difficult to lather soap in, is rich in magnesium and calcium salts. When the water is heated to 71°C (about 160°F) it deposits fur or scale on the inside of pipes, radiators and cisterns – the same kind of deposit as seen inside a kettle.

In a central heating system with a direct HOT WATER CYLINDER, scale can reduce the effective bore of pipework and promote inefficient heating. A water softener, containing a synthetic softening agent, can be permanently connected to the RISING MAIN, supplying softened water to all taps. Alternatively, a portable softener can be used, connected to a tap by a rubber hose, to soften water where and when it is required.

WATT The unit measurement of electricity. One kilowatt is 1000 watts and 1 kW burning for one hour consumes one unit of electricity.

(◗ AMPERE; VOLT)

WEATHER BAR A length of moulded softwood, rebated into the outer face of a door, so that the underside of both are flush.

The bar helps to reduce draughts and throw off rainwater.

WEATHER-BOARDING Softwood boards nailed to BATTENS fixed to the outer face of a wall – timber-framed, brick or building blocks – to provide a weatherproof WALL CLADDING.

Weather boarding may be done with plain square-edge boards, feather-edge (wedge-shaped) boards, REBATED boards (where each interlocks with its neighbour), and SHIPLAP boarding.

WEATHERING The inclined surface on the top of stone sills, CORNICES, STRING COURSES, and so on, shaped to throw off rainwater.

Also known as a water table or offset.

Weathering also describes the effect the weather has on building materials.

WEDGE A tapered piece of wood used to force materials apart or to apply pressure for a temporary fixing, such as when hanging a door.
(◗ FOLDING WEDGES)

WEEP HOLES Vertical brick joints above a door or window that are left without mortar in them in order to allow moisture in a cavity to seep out.

Also, the small holes that are sometimes drilled down and out through a window sill to allow moisture – formed by condensation – to escape.

WELT A folded seam between adjoining sheets of metal roof covering, such as lead or zinc.

WET AND DRY ◗ ABRASIVES

WET ROT A form of timber decay caused by fungi.
(Coniophora cerebella) that attacks damp wood found in unventilated places, such as cellars and attics. Unlike DRY ROT, if the dampness is eradicated, the wood will dry out and no further decay will occur; but the damaged wood will have to be replaced and all remaining timber treated with a PRESERVATIVE.

Mild attacks of wet rot can be treated by the handyman but a serious outbreak should be dealt with only by a specialist.

WHEELBRACE ◗ DRILLS

WHITE LEAD ◗ PUTTY

WHITE METER ◗ OFF-PEAK TARIFF

WHITE SAND ◗ SAND

WHITE SPIRIT ◗ TURPENTINE SUBSTITUTE

WHITEWOOD FURNITURE Inexpensive furniture made from a light white/yellow coloured wood having a tight close grain. Also known as white deal, yellow pine, common spruce, Norway spruce, spruce fir and, in Scotland, white pine.

WIDE-ANGLE HINGE ◗ HINGES

WIGGLE NAIL ◆ CORRUGATED FASTENER

WIND FILLING Bricks carried up between the roofing JOISTS on a wall to seal the EAVES.

WINDOW BARS ◆ GLAZING BARS

WINDOW BOARD A wooden shelf-like sill on the inside of a window.

WINDOWS ◆ CASEMENT; EYEBROW WINDOW; FIXED LIGHT; FRENCH WINDOW; LEADED LIGHT; METAL WINDOWS; OPENING LIGHTS; ORIEL WINDOW; SASH, SASH BAR; SASH CORD; VENETIAN WINDOW; WINDOW BARS; WINDOW BOARD

WING NUT A nut with two 'wings' so that it can be tightened by hand.

WIPED JOINT A traditional technique used for jointing lead pipes. One of the pipes to be joined is widened slightly at the neck to receive the other, which is tapered to fit into it. The pipes are then shaved clean (with a SHAVEHOOK) and painted with PLUMBER'S BLACK beyond the line of the joint. They are then joined with SOLDER and while still wet wiped by hand with a fustian – moleskin – cloth, to form a swollen connection that is smoothly 'feathered' at the edges.

WIRE BALLOON A spherical cage, made of GALVANIZED steel wire, that fits into the top of a VENTILATING PIPE or a gutter outlet to prevent leaves causing blockages.

WIRE CUTS ◆ BRICKS

WIRED GLASS ◆ GLASS

WIRE NAIL ◆ NAILS

WIRE STRIPPERS ◆ PLIERS

WIRE WOOL ◆ ABRASIVES

WOODBLOCK FLOORING Strips of hardwood from 6 mm to 16 mm ($\frac{1}{4}$ in. to $\frac{5}{8}$ in.) thick used to surface concrete or timber sub-floors.

The hardwood strips may be BUTT-JOINTED or TONGUED-AND-GROOVED, and fixed to concrete floors with adhesive, and to timber floors with adhesive and PANEL PINS.

There are also various types of proprietary hardwood flooring systems that are particularly easy for the amateur to lay. They basically consist of pieces of hardwood, such as teak or mahogany, glued to convenient-sized backing sheets of tongued-and-grooved CHIPBOARD, softwood, BITUMINIZED FELT, or cotton scrim.

Panel sizes vary from small units roughly 115 mm (4½ ins.) square to 485 mm (about 19 ins.) square.

The strips of timber may be arranged in herringbone, basketweave or parquet bonds.

WOODCHIP PAPER ♦ WALLPAPERS
WOODEN FLOAT ♦ FLOATS
WOODWOOL SLABS Prefabricated material in slab form, with fire-resistant, acoustic and thermal insulation properties.

The slabs are made from long shavings of wood, compressed and mixed with cement. Used for walls and roofs – generally as part of a sandwich construction, i.e. in conjunction with other materials.

WOODWORM The majority of damage done by woodworm, in structural timbers as well as furniture, is caused by the common furniture beetle (*Anobium punctatum*). The beetle lays its eggs in crevices in the wood's surface, the eggs hatch into grubs, and the grubs bore their way into the wood for a period of three to four years, weakening the timber in the process. When the grub finally emerges as an adult beetle the damage has already been done. The exit holes are about 2 mm ($\frac{1}{16}$ in.) in diameter, surrounded by flour-like dust.

Mild attacks can be treated with insecticide but doubtful or serious outbreaks must be dealt with by a specialist.

The death-watch beetle (*Xestobium rufovillosum*) is rarely found in modern houses; it is largely confined to structural hardwoods in old buildings where dampness and a lack of adequate ventilation have led to fungal decay. They burrow into the wood, leaving circular holes about 3 mm ($\frac{1}{8}$ in.) in diameter, surrounded by pellets of dust. The adults make a clicking noise once thought to predict death – hence the name.

Once the cause of decay has been cured the timber must be impregnated with a chemical insecticide. Again it is a job best left to the specialist.

WORKING DRAWINGS Plans, elevations, sections and full-size details of a building, drawn to a convenient scale by an architect, surveyor or designer for a builder to estimate, and price and build from.

Working drawings and a SPECIFICATION often constitute the principal CONTRACT documents.

WRENCHES (MONKEY GRIPS) Similar to adjustable spanners, but generally capable of applying considerably greater pressures, and therefore suitable for gripping pipework or shifting a damaged nut.

Adjustable wrenches (except the torque wrench) have one fixed and one opening jaw – both with serrated teeth for biting into a workpiece. Force should always be applied in the direction of the movable jaw in order to gain the maximum leverage.

The principle types are:
Basin An extra-long-handled wrench for use in constricted spaces, such as when working on the underside of a bath or basin.

Sizes of jaw width open up to 50 mm (2 ins.).

Pipe (Stilson) A heavyweight tool with spring-loaded jaws and a fine-adjustment mechanism for gripping steel pipework or similar heavyweight metals. It is unsuitable for copper pipework which may be crushed by the wrench.

adjustable

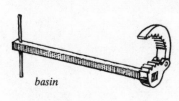

basin

pipe wrench

WRENCHES

Self-grip (Mole) A wrench that can be locked on to a workpiece with considerable pressure and remain in place, unsupported, leaving the hands free until a release mechanism is operated.

self grip

Types vary from manufacturer to manufacturer, designed to suit different shapes and metal.

Sizes from 125 mm to 300 mm (5 ins. to 12 ins.).

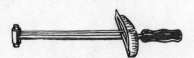

Torque A wrench with a measuring gauge on it that enables the user to apply the correct pressure when tightening nuts, e.g. when tightening the nuts on a car engine's cylinder head.

(◆ SPANNERS)

WROT Planed timber. Also known as wrought timber.

Y

YALE LOCK ▸ LOCKS
YANKEE SCREWDRIVER ▸ SCREW-
DRIVERS